I AM YOUR MOTHER

COME FROM HEAVEN

TO LOVE YOU

Heavenly messages for the family

Printed in the USA by
Z'Atelier® Publications
Plano, TX 75023-1710

The publisher recognizes and accepts that the final authority regarding the spiritual or heavenly authorship of the messages given to Janie Garza rests with the Holy See of Rome, Italy. The publisher willingly submits to the final judgment/decision of the Holy See in this matter.

First edition, English, October 1994

Copyright restrictions are not intended to prevent the dissemination of the materials protected by the copyright(s) and will be enforced for the intentional or non-intentional misrepresentation(s) of these materials.

DEDICATION

This book is dedicated to the Holy Family, who during these past five years, have helped me to love and embrace my family, to our beloved Pope, John Paul II, who has declared 1994 as the "International Year of the Family," and to my husband Marcelino and my family, without whom this book would not be.

Janie Garza
Austin, Texas

PREFACE

Robert L. Fastiggi, Ph.D., Associate Professor of Religious Studies, St. Edward's University, Austin, Texas

"The future of humanity passes by way of the family". These words of Pope John Paul II, given in his 1981 Apostolic Exhortation on "The Role of the Christian Family in the Modern World: (Familiaris consortio), provide a fitting context for this book of beautiful messages given to Janie Garza between the years 1989 and 1994. We all know that the family is under attack by the forces of evil. The rise in divorce, spousal violence and child abuse - all point to a situation which makes supernatural intervention both appropriate and credible. It also seems providential that a book like this should be published in 1994, the International Year of the Family. His Holiness, Pope John Paul II, has highlighted the importance of the family in the recent beatifications of Elizabeth Canori Mora and Gianna Beretta Molla - two devout women who, like Janie Garza, pursued holiness as wives and mothers, even in the midst of much pain and struggle.

"Blessed are the pure in heart, for they will see God (Mat. 5:8)" - this Scripture seems to be the guiding light of these messages. Mary, speaking under the title of Mother of Compassion and Love, tells Janie: "Be loving, be prayerful, be obedient. Pray for purity of heart, for when you pray with a pure heart, God answers your prayers. He loves purity (August 15, 1992)." Prayer and purity of heart emerge as two of the most important themes in these messages along with a special emphasis on the need for family prayer as the remedy for the problems which exist in all too many households. By praying together family members draw closer to each other and to God. Praying the Rosary is especially recommended since it provides a powerful protection against the assaults of Satan who is intent on destroying as many families as he can. All this confirms the teachings of the recent Popes who have recommended the family Rosary "with particular solicitude and insistence (Famliaris consortio, 61)."

While it is not my role to provide official ecclesiastical approval of the supernatural character of these messages, I think it is fair to say that they present a series of exhortations and recommendations which are in perfect harmony with the Scriptures and the Catholic faith. The themes that are repeatedly stressed - prayer, purity of heart, conversion, fasting, compassion, forgiveness, mercy, detachment,

i

trust in God, patient endurance and abandonment to the Immaculate Heart of Mary and the Sacred Heart of Jesus - resonate not only with approved Marian apparitions (e.g. Fatima) but also with the spirituality of many great saints and mystics (e.g. St. Theresa of Avila, St. John Eudes, Jean-Pierre de Caussade and St. Therese of Lisieux). In terms of human faith, I find it quite credible that Janie Garza, a woman whose heart has been purified through much suffering, would be the type of humble soul that God would choose to grace with interior visions and locutions containing messages of particular importance for our time.

One of the extraordinary qualities of this book is the way it links the domestic Church of the home with the universal Church. This is manifested by the geographic movement of the messages from their origin in the simplicity of Janie's home in Austin, Texas to their eventual reception in places like New Orleans, Detroit, Mexico, Lourdes, Lisbon, Rome, Prague and Red Square in Moscow. This incredible odyssey, guided it seems by supernatural Providence, eventually returns to the home. The lesson is that Mary's "prayer warriors," gathered together on a pilgrimage to the ends of the earth, must return to their individual families to build up the reign of peace in the domestic Church of the home. Prayer in each family is the spiritual precondition for world peace and the renewal of the universal Church.

Another extraordinary quality of this book is the way the prayer life of the family on earth is supported by the supernatural guidance of the Holy Family of Jesus, Mary and Joseph (since Janie receives messages from all three). The involvement of angels and the exhortations to pray for the souls in Purgatory highlight the importance of linking the individual family to the larger family of the Mystical Body of Christ which includes the faithful on earth, the souls in Purgatory and the angels and saints in heaven.

A number of themes are also stressed which seem to resonate with other reported messages of this age. Jesus ,speaks to Janie from His Eucharistic Heart, and the importance of Eucharistic devotion is highlighted. Prayers for priests are urged by Mary because many priests have grown weak in their faith and are resisting the authority of the Pope.

Fidelity to the Holy Father is stressed by Mary, and she refers to the Pontiff as "my beloved Pope." Several references are made to the urgency of the present times, the activity of Satan in the world and the need to prepare for the tribulation. Although the dangers of too much television, materialism and sexual immorality are noted, abortion seems to be singled out as the "horrible evil" of this age.

While a sense of urgency is present in these messages, there is also a pervasive exhortation to trust in God and not to worry or be anxious. While Mary does identify herself to Janie as the Mother of Sorrows on some occasions, she most frequently appears as the Mother of Compassion and Love who urges her children to seek refuge in the warmth of her Immaculate Heart and the mercy of her Son's Sacred Heart. When Jesus speaks, there is an ever-present sense of love and tenderness and He makes clear to Janie: "I am here for you always. I have given you My Precious Body and Blood so you would be redeemed. Take My Body and be nourished. Take My Blood and do not thirst. I am your strength. I am your hope. I am your teacher. (October 22, 1991)."

Beginning in 1993, messages from St. Joseph become more frequent, and the great saint gives special instructions for husbands to be chaste, prayerful, pure, gentle, loving, obedient and humble. St. Joseph also urges wives to pray for the virtues of purity, obedience and humility. He counsels children to be pure and chaste, obedient to their parents and prayerful in their choice of friends and careers. A beautiful prayer to St. Joseph is given to Janie, along with other inspired prayers given for family consecrations to the Holy Spirit, the Immaculate Heart of Mary and the Sacred Heart of Jesus. Prayers to St. Michael the Archangel and to the Holy Spirit are given special encouragement, along with daily recitation of the Rosary and the wearing of the Scapular.

It is clear from these messages, that prayer and purity of heart are central to the renewal of the family, the priesthood and the Church. The attacks of Satan against the sanctity of the family and the priesthood give these messages a special urgency and a special credibility. While the assaults of the evil one appear to be on the increase, the Mother of Compassion and Love tells us: "Do not have the smallest worry or fear, for I, your heavenly Mother, am with each one of you. I protect all my children through my motherly mantle. Take refuge in my Son's Sacred Heart and in my Most Immaculate Heart, for in the Two United Hearts you will find your safety. Every day, consecrate your lives to the Two Hearts and no harm will come to you as a family (July 20, 1993)."

There is a beautiful simplicity to the messages of this book, a simplicity which is at once direct and profound. The essence of these messages can only be appreciated by those willing to accept the way of spiritual childhood - those who are willing to become like little children in order to enter the Kingdom of Heaven (Mat. 18:3).

While it is not within my competence to confirm these messages as supernatural in character, I do feel confident to recommend this book for spiritual inspiration and prayerful reflection. The pure and humble quality of Janie Garza's soul breathes through every page of this book. However, as Janie would be the first to admit, our focus should not be on her, but on the Immaculate Heart of Mary and the Sacred Heart of Jesus united as a secure refuge of mercy and compassion in a world crying out for love.

Robert L. Fastiggi, Ph.D.
Associate Professor of Religious Studies
St. Edward's University, Austin, Texas

INTRODUCTION

Rev. Henry Bordeaux, O.C.D., Dallas, Texas

"Give evidence of your deeds of old, fulfill the prophecies spoken in your name, reward those who have hoped in you, and let your prophets be proven true. Hear the prayer of your servants, for you are ever gracious to your people, thus it will be known to the very ends of the earth that you are the eternal God." (Sirach 36, 14-17)

This selection of an Old Testament prayer finds an echo in the souls of numerous Christian families today, as they experience the fierce tugging of the world and the evil one.

Indeed, the family is being assaulted today as never before. The mentality of the world has seeped into families bringing with it divorce, fighting, lack of discipline and forgiveness; driving out family prayer and a humble spirit which seeks wisdom not from the world, but from the infallible Word of God and the sure teachings of His Church.

Many are the prophets whom the Holy Spirit has raised up today to teach us the true and divine plan for the family. The chief prophet in the Church today is John Paul II, our saintly and courageous Pope, who speaks so clearly with divine wisdom about our families and what is God's Will for them.

Mrs. Janie Garza of Austin, Texas, wife and mother, was chosen by the Lord to be a vessel of simple and holy messages for the family of today. These messages are given by the Holy Family - Jesus, Mary and Joseph. Messengers like St. Michael the Archangel are also mentioned.

Janie has been receiving messages since February 15, 1989. I can testify that since I became her spiritual director nearly two years ago, I have seen immense growth in virtue in her, in her husband and in her sons, two of whom are teenagers.

The purpose of these messages is no doubt to help Christian families become holy families. Thus, Our Lady teaches us from her own experience as wife and mother, being of course full of grace.

v

The great St. Joseph gives us sublime teachings on the family, coming from his own experience as husband and foster father of the Divine Infant. His soul, so full of love for his Divine Foster Child and his wife, and so full of God's wisdom, makes his teachings fresh and absorbing for husbands and wives, fathers and mothers and for the young, too.

As Janie Garza's spiritual director, I have never found anything in all the messages which in any way goes against any teaching of our Holy Catholic Church. I have seen the profound effects these messages have had in others when they read them or have heard Janie speak. So, together with her two previous spiritual directors, I have, after years of prayer for discernment and wisdom, affirmed that these messages are of heavenly origin. I wish, however, to quickly add that I, together with Janie and Marcelino, her husband, submit our judgment to our Holy Catholic Church.

Particular points raised by Our Lady are family prayer, the great power of the Rosary, the Sacraments of Penance and Eucharist, a return to God and devotion to her Immaculate Heart and her Son's Sacred Heart. She always speaks as a tender Mother, but warns us of the dangers of the present age and the supreme importance of living her messages.

Let the reader partake of this rich fare. Each particular family, each parish family, and the family of the Church (the family of man also) can greatly profit from these enlightening instructions.

The Garza family and I thank the Holy Family for the greatness of their love and compassion. May Our Mother of Compassion and Love, who appears to Janie under this title, accept our love and gratitude and through the powerful prayers of her husband, St. Joseph, lead us to complete unity with Jesus Christ, who is Lord of Lords and King of Kings. Amen.

Rev. Henry Bordeaux, O.C.D.
Dallas, Texas

PROLOGUE

Medjugorje, June 23, 1994

Our Lady's words: "My child, on my thirteenth anniversary, you will receive the title for your book. My Son will tell you the title. Trust Him."

Medjugorje, June 25, 1994

Our Lord's words: "My little flower, recall My Mothers' first words to you. This will be the title for your book. Embrace this title."

Austin, Texas, February 26, 1989

Our Lady's first words: "I am your Mother come from Heaven to love you."

CONTENTS

MESSAGES

I am Your Mother Come from Heaven to Love You

Message from Our Lady, February 26, 1989

I saw Our Lady during my prayer, I asked her, "Who are you?"

She replied, "I am your Mother come from Heaven to love you."

Then I asked, "Do you have a name?"

Our Lady replied, "To you, my child, I come as The Lady of the Rosary, and I charge you and your family with this mission: to go out and bring living Rosaries for my Son, Jesus."

I did not understand this message. I thought my family and I were to make Rosaries. I prayed for enlightenment.

I am Your Mother Come from Heaven to Love You

Message from Our Lady, February 27, 1989

Our Lady said to me, "My child, I come to teach you how to be a loving wife and to help you to be submissive to your husband."

I rebuked these words, just in case it may have been the devil lying to me. I felt that God knew that I had never been submissive to anyone!

Our Lady continued speaking, "My child, your husband is very special to God. He is gentle, kind and loving. He is a good provider and a good father. He has a gentle heart."

At this point I asked, "Blessed Mother, are we talking about the same man I married?"

She smiled and said, "Yes, my child, yes. My child, when you submit to your husband, you help him to submit to God. Trust me, my child, and allow me to teach you all about being a prayerful and loving family - the kind of family that God intended for you to be."

I am Your Mother Come from Heaven to Love You

Message from Our Lady, February 27, 1989
While praying the Rosary.

Our Lady said to me, "My child, whenever Satan is disturbing you, pray your Rosary. When your family is undergoing much suffering, pray your Rosary. Whenever you want to lead others to God, pray your Rosary.

Through praying the Rosary those souls that you are praying for will begin to change. Through the Rosary they will come closer to God, and they will have a desire to want to convert; but you must pray very hard. My child, there is much healing through praying the Rosary, and I am always present when my children pray their Rosaries."

I am Your Mother Come from Heaven to Love You

Message from Our Lady, February 27, 1989

Our Lady said to me, "My child, be patient with your husband and pray for him. Offer all your own struggles and sufferings for his conversion.

Accept your family with unconditional love. Teach them about the love of God and help them to pray with you. Do not become discouraged when your family refuses to pray with you. Be gentle, patient and loving with them.

My child, you will suffer much for your family's conversion. As you suffer for them, your own heart will begin to convert. Pray, pray, pray."

Message from Our Lady, February 28, 1989

Our Lady said to me, "My child, I will teach you how to pray your Rosary with love in your heart. Through your devotion to praying your Rosary, you will help others in your family to convert.

My child, I ask that you add this prayer when you begin your Rosary:

My God, I believe, I adore, I hope and I love You. I beg pardon of you, for those who do not believe, do not adore, do not hope and do not love You.

My child, do not worry about your family; through your prayers they are drawing closer to my Son."

Later on this same day, Our Lady said to me, "Continue to pray for your family and pray and fast for these intentions."

4

I am Your Mother Come from Heaven to Love You

Message from Our Lord Jesus, March 17, 1989

Jesus spoke to me while I was visiting the Blessed Sacrament:

My dear child, I, your Jesus of Love and Mercy speak to your heart. Do not be concerned about your husband. Be loving and patient with him and be gentle. Be forgiving, for he is trying to understand more about being prayerful. Give him to Me and allow Me to help you both.

Remain loving and obedient, and through your attitude your family will pray more. You will suffer much for much is being asked of you by My Father in Heaven, for you have found much favor with My Father.

Message from Our Lord Jesus, March 18, 1989

Jesus spoke to me while I was visiting the Blessed Sacrament:

My child, listen to My beloved Mother and do all that she is asking of you. Through your obedience to her and to Me your prayer will convert many families.

My child, you have such a great love for the Rosary. Pray every day!

I am Your Mother Come from Heaven to Love You

Message from Our Lady, March 20, 1989

Our Lady said to me, "My child, continue praying your Rosary for peace in your heart and for peace in your family. Pray for peace in the world and for the conversion of my daughter, Russia, for she is in need of much conversion. Offer your prayers for the most distant souls and for the Holy Souls in Purgatory. Pray for conversion throughout the world.

My child, when you pray with your family, offer up your prayers for my special intention. When the faithful pray with faith in their hearts, they will begin to see changes in their hearts and in their families. Sinners will convert, wars will cease, and my Son will begin to live in many new hearts. Teach your family how to pray with faith and love in their hearts."

Message from Our Lady, March 23, 1989

Our Lady said to me, "My child, continue to pray with your family, for soon you will see their hearts change. Healing of woundedness of heart will be one of the results, the fruits of your prayers."

Message from Our Lady, March 24, 1989

Our Lady said to me, "My child, I am praying with you, and I am blessing your family in a special way. Your son is on his way to recovery, continue to pray for him."

Later on that day, my son told me that he felt the love of Our Lady. My family was unaware that Our Lady is visiting me!

I am Your Mother Come from Heaven to Love You

Message from Our Lord Jesus, April 5, 1989

I was praying about some concerns that I had, when Jesus said to me, "My child, fear nothing, put your trust in Me."

Message from Our Lady, April 5, 1989
Given at the church

Our Lady said, "My child, why are you troubled? Why are you afraid? Haven't I told you that I am with you?" I began to cry to hear her say this to me.

Then she said, "My child, why the tears? Believe in your heart that I am with you. I called you here, so that I could console your heart and to tell you that your prayers have been heard.

My little child, I know you are suffering. Do not be afraid. You have the protection and guidance of my Son and the enlightenment of my Spouse, the Holy Spirit. Your Guardian Angel is also with you at all times. He is protecting you.

My child, I know that you want to be healed from what you are going through. In just a short time you will be healed, but not now. Know that through your suffering you are being purified, for God Himself is calling you to purity. Offer up your suffering in reparation for your own conversion and for your family's conversion.

Be at peace, my child, and dry your tears. Go out and enjoy this beautiful day with your husband."

I am Your Mother Come from Heaven to Love You

Message from Our Lady, April 8, 1989

Today, I had not prayed my Rosary.

When Our Lady came, she spoke these words, "My child, what is wrong? Why haven't you prayed your Rosary today? Don't you know how important it is to pray the Rosary daily? My child, I want your prayers, so that through your prayers you can help souls to convert."

I apologized to her and prayed my Rosary.

Message from Our Lady, April 8, 1989

Our Lady to me, "My child, I will guide you as you pray for your family. I will teach you about intercessory prayer. I will teach you about the angels and saints and how they can help you. I will lead you and your family closer to my Son."

Since Our Lady began to visit me, I have much more peace. I am calm. I have a joy I've never known before. For this I am grateful to God.

Message from Our Lady, April 14, 1989

I was doubting my experiences of Our Lady speaking to my heart.

Our Lady said to me, "My child, believe in your heart that I, your heavenly Mother, have chosen to speak to you interiorly. I speak to your heart. I speak to my children in many ways. Some hear my voice, others see me and hear my voice. Others only hear my voice as an interior voice. This is the way that I speak to you. Be at peace, and do not be overcome with doubt."

I am Your Mother Come from Heaven to Love You

Message from Our Lady, April 15, 1989

During prayer I was telling Our Lady how happy I was, because I had her as my Mother. I was thanking her for loving me. Her words to me, "My child, yes, I do love you, but you also love me and I, your heavenly Mother, responded to your love.

My child, you have been devoted to praying your Rosary, and through praying your Rosary you demonstrated your love to me. Please share this beautiful devotion with your family. Share with your family that conversion is obtained through praying the Rosary. My children (your family) will be blessed and healings will take place in their hearts. Pray your Rosary every day for conversion in your own life."

Preparing to tell my family, May 1, 1989

I spent the month of May praying and preparing for a priest whom Our Lady asked me to pray for. This month was also the month in which I was to talk to my family concerning Our Lady speaking to my heart. I was very nervous and afraid of my family's reaction. In a way I was hoping that this moment would never come. All that Mary had told me, I was praying about. I prayed about everything. Jesus and Our Lady were being so gentle with me.

I am Your Mother Come from Heaven to Love You

Our Lady Gives me a Priest to tell about my Visitations
June 1, 1989

Today, Our Lady gave me the priest that I am to talk to concerning my visitations. I am growing more and more nervous. I called to make an appointment for Monday at 3:00 p.m.. Tomorrow I'll go to San Antonio, Texas for a private retreat. My friend invited me. I guess this is how Our Lady will prepare me.

I met with my family in the last part of May to share with them about my visitations. I think they believed me. I don't know, but they sure were being nice to me. Maybe they thought I'd lost it!

Our Lady will begin to teach us as a family now. So far she's been teaching me about submission and obedience.

Message from Our Lady, June 4, 1989

Tonight, I wanted to tear up everything and cancel the appointment with Father. I wanted to stop praying and forget everything. Our Lady came to me, and she showed me a green meadow. Then before my eyes it turned brown; then it was all dark and burnt.

Her words, "This is how your own soul will become if you stop praying.

June 5, 1989

Today, I met with Father. I was so scared, but Our Lady helped me. Father said that he believed that what I was receiving were divine messages from Jesus and Mary. He asked me to leave everything that I have written with him. I am so nervous!

I am Your Mother Come from Heaven to Love You

June 18, 1989

I received everything back today from Father. He said it was of divine origin. I can't believe it. He agreed to be my Spiritual Director and to see me once a week or more, as I need to see him.

Message from Our Lady, June 21, 1989

Our Lady to me, "My child, your prayers and efforts are good, but you have not been focused on your commitment to help your family with their prayers. You have not been praying as much, and you have been impatient with your family.

My child, you must have a loving attitude when helping your family. You have allowed your anger to dominate you.

My child, I know that you are suffering (I have a physical problem), but I will help you through this rough period. Offer all your pain for conversion in your family. Have a loving attitude and pray with faith in your heart. Through your prayers, fasting and sufferings, many others than your family will be converted.

Do not worry about anything, but write everything I tell you. God has many blessings for your family. He is calling you to bring other families to Him through praying your Rosary. Teach others the importance of praying the Rosary as a family. My child, I will come and visit with you again soon."

I am Your Mother Come from Heaven to Love You

Message from Our Lady, July 28, 1989
Preparing for Mass at the Blessed Sacrament

REGARDING THE IMPORTANCE OF
PRAYING THE ROSARY BEFORE MASS

My child, I invite you to pray the Rosary before Holy Mass. In this way, you will be an example to others. I invite my children to spend fifteen minutes praying their Rosary, to help them to prepare for Holy Mass.

If my children respond to my request, God will heal their wounded hearts. Conversion will be easy for those who want to convert. When my children pray the Rosary together, they begin to heal as a community. God's peace begins to flow as my children pray the Rosary.

Message from Our Lady, August 30, 1989

My dear children, I, your heavenly Mother, invite you to be filled with God's peace. You have my gratitude for praying your Rosary together as a family.

My children, do not forget the importance of family prayer, especially the family Rosary. When you pray as a family, you grow as a family. Do not be afraid to convert, but convert! I will help you and lead you, as a family, closer to my Son, Jesus.

Open your hearts to my Son's Most Sacred Heart and to my Most Immaculate Heart, and decide for conversion. Pray for world peace, for there is so much pain, suffering and corruption due to lack of faith. Be open to my Son's love and mercy and share His love and mercy with others by reaching to the unconverted souls. Pray, my children, pray.

I am Your Mother Come from Heaven to Love You

Message from Our Lady, August 31, 1989

My child, continue to pray and do all that my Son invites you to do. Do not be concerned with anything. You are protected by the Two United Hearts.

My child, do not be without your Scapular, for it is my garment of grace, and you are under my protection. Never be without it!

Message from Our Lord Jesus in the Blessed Sacrament
August 31, 1989

My child, welcome to My Eucharistic Heart. I have missed your visits. Thank you for coming to spend time with Me. Today, My child, I want to share My sadness with you.

My children do not come to visit with Me. I spend hours alone, and very few come. Sometimes no one comes. My child, I turn to you and ask you to invite others to come to visit Me. I will refresh their souls, I will heal their wounded hearts. I will renew their hearts, and they will be filled with My peace.

I have so much love to give My children. Invite them to come and spend time with the One Who loves them more than anyone else. Thank you, My child, for all your prayers.

I am Your Mother Come from Heaven to Love You

Message from Our Lady, September 2, 1989
First Saturday

GUIDANCE ON THE POWER OF WEARING THE SCAPULAR

Today, I had a question concerning taking my Scapular off while I was showering, since Our Lady asked me to wear the Scapular and never be without it. I prayed, and then Our Lady came. I did not see her dressed in white. She came in brown and cream. She came with a crown on her head and a Child in her arms. I asked her what her name was under this title.

Then, before my eyes, I saw her in different attires. I didn't recognize all of them, only a few. Our Lady of Guadeloupe, the Immaculate Conception, Our Lady of the Rosary, and Our Lady of San Juan were the only titles I recognized.

After this, I again saw Our Lady in brown and cream with a crown on her head and the Christ Child in her arms. I understood that she was appearing to me under the title of Our Lady of Mount Carmel. She spoke these words: "My child, I have allowed you to see me in many different titles, but I am the same Mother of God and Mother of All Creation. I come to my children in the titles that they can relate to me as their heavenly Mother.

Continue praying for the conversion of your family. Your commitment to your prayers brings so much joy to my Immaculate Heart.

My child, regarding wearing your Scapular, wear it always, for through wearing your Scapular you are protected from many evils during the day."

I am Your Mother Come from Heaven to Love You

Message from Our Lady, September 10, 1989

My children, you bring joy to my Immaculate Heart as you pray your family Rosary. Pray together as a family, and you will be strong during trials and tribulations.

My children, some of you are suffering and have wounded hearts. Do not worry, I am here to protect you and to lead you closer to my Son, Jesus.

Message from Our Lady to my family, November 30, 1989

My dear children, I invite you to open your hearts to my Son Who loves you. Do not reject His love, but turn to Him and accept His love. Be converted, be converted! Love one another and continue to pray together as a family. Know, my children, that you are special to me, and I hold you all to my motherly bosom.

I invite you to trust in my motherly intercession, so that I may lead you all to purity of heart. Take refuge in my Most Immaculate Heart, and I will help you to remain strong during hard times.

My children, continue to pray together, and remember, the Rosary is your weapon. Pray, pray, pray! When you are under Satan's attack and you cannot pray your Rosary, pray one Hail Mary; this sends Satan running. He hates prayer.

I am Your Mother Come from Heaven to Love You

Message from Our Lady, December 7, 1989
Family Rosary

Tonight, I say thank you all for praying together as a family.

My children, some of you are hurting. You are worried about Christmas, and you have no money to give gifts. Give the gift of love that comes from your heart. Prepare your hearts for the birth of my Son and allow Him to be born in your own heart. Do not be sad my children. God wants to bless you. Dry your tears and be open to God's love. It saddens my heart to see you sad. Pray with your heavenly Mother, and you will receive God's peace.

My children, tonight, I invite you to trust in my intercession especially in this holy season, so that I may help you to prepare your hearts for the birth of my Son.

Message from Our Lady, December 14, 1989
Family Rosary

My children, tonight, I thank you for coming together for prayer. I invite you to trust God with all your family concerns.

Again, I invite you to allow me to help you during this holy season. Do not be concerned with all the distractions concerning gifts, but offer your love to one another; this is the best gift of all.

Continue to pray and have no worry, but rejoice. My children, you are seeking answers to prayers, and some of you are becoming discouraged. Open your hearts and abandon yourselves to God. Give Him all your burdens. God is listening to all your prayers. Do not give up but continue to pray, for prayer is your strength.

Tonight, Our Lady said we were receiving special healing of our hearts.

I am Your Mother Come from Heaven to Love You

Message from Our Lady, January 4, 1990
Family Neighborhood Rosary

My children, tonight, there are some of you who are suffering, and your hearts are sad. I, your heavenly Mother, invite you to pray and meditate on the Glorious Mysteries with joy in your hearts.

My children, many of you are worried about your own children, and some of you have children who are not praying. Pray for them and trust in your prayers. Leave all your worries and sadness at God's disposal. If you do this, all will go well with your children.

I welcome all my children who are here, and I invite you to open your hearts to your heavenly Mother. Know, my children, that I have called each one of you to be here and to pray your Rosary together.

My children, do not give up hope when you are suffering, but turn to my Immaculate Heart. I want to protect you all; that is why I ask that you trust your heavenly Mother. I do not want you to be sad when you are overcome by failure, but continue to pray for God's strength. Never give up, my children, but pray unceasingly!

My children, I invite you to accept me as your heavenly Mother and to accept my love. I know that it is difficult to live a good life; that is why I invite you to abandon yourselves to my Immaculate Heart. I will help you to endure your crosses with love.

My children, I invite you to commit every morning to make a sacrifice to pray more for your family. Prayer will be your strength. Begin and end each day with prayer, for prayer brings you peace.

My children, if you only understood how much you are loved by God, you would open your hearts. You must become totally dependent on God for everything; in this way you will be able to accept all your trials and sufferings with joy. God will see to all your needs. Trust Him.

I am Your Mother Come from Heaven to Love You

Message from Our Lady, Queen of Mercy
(I did not recognize this title)
Neighborhood Family Rosary, January 11, 1990

My children, tonight, I come to console each one of you. My heart is sorrowful for many of you who are suffering and have stopped praying. Some of you are doubting in the blessings that you are receiving."

I asked, "What would make you happy my Lady?"

"My children, open your hearts and pray. This will bring joy to my heart."

Our Lady to me, "My child, pray to the Holy Spirit, and He will open the door to your heart."

I saw myself at her feet. She placed both hands on my head. I said to her, "Dear Lady, I do not want you to be sad."

She responded, "Pray, my child, pray."

"My children, pray the Rosary with joy. Tonight I bless each one present and I bless all your intentions."

All the families, gathered tonight, felt the presence of Our Lady.

Message from Our Lady, January 18, 1990

My children, tonight, I invite you to prepare your hearts before you pray your Rosary. (She wanted us to be silent instead of visiting before praying the Rosary).

My children, pray your Rosary with love and faith in your hearts. Tonight, many of you are afflicted with illness and viruses. I ask that you offer up all your suffering for peace in your family.

18

I am Your Mother Come from Heaven to Love You

Message from Our Lady, January 18, 1990 (Continued)

My children, I am aware that many of you are ill. Continue praying and know that I am praying with you. Love one another and open the doors to your hearts from within. (She meant that our hearts are not open to receive one another's love).

My children, pray for all your neighbors and for the needs of the world. Pray especially for the youth; they are in great need of prayer! Be strong, my children, and arm yourselves through prayer, for Satan will destroy you if you are not praying. Do not be afraid, for I am protecting you. I am teaching you about praying as a family and the importance of loving one another.

Pray your Rosary every day. Some of you are feeling overcome by your crosses and tribulations, especially in your family. My children, the reason that you are feeling this way is because you are praying without faith in your hearts. Pray, my children, pray.

Message from Our Lady, January 22, 1990
Neighborhood Family Rosary

My children, tonight, I invite you to pray, so that through your prayers others will come to God.

My children, I call you to prayer of the heart, where you abandon all totally to God. Satan is busy trying to destroy you, but through prayer you will conquer everything.

My children, I, your heavenly Mother, have come to teach you how to love with God's love. Open your hearts, open your hearts. How can I help you if you do not pray? Ask the Lord for the grace to be strong through your prayers.

I bless you all, my children, and I extend my love to each one. You have struggled to come together for prayer, but you remain committed, and I thank you.

19

I am Your Mother Come from Heaven to Love You

Message from Our Lady, January 25, 1990
Neighborhood Family Rosary

My children, tonight, I, your heavenly Mother, thank you all for coming to pray together as a family.

My children, I bring you peace. Do not be concerned about your troubles, for I, your Mother, am with you. Do not be afraid.

Little children, there are many needs here tonight. Through prayer and fasting you will receive the answers to your prayers and the answers that you are seeking. Open your hearts, for I have come to bring you peace.

My children, some of you are worried about finances. Do not worry; God has heard your prayers. Some of you are doubting; do not doubt. Keep your eyes on my Son, Jesus. He will help you not to become discouraged.

My children, I am happy for many of my young people are being committed to prayer. To you, I invite you to pray your Rosary every day.

My children, do not get upset with others who do not pray or have faith. Pray for them and invite them to come to pray.

Message from Our Lady, February 8, 1990
Neighborhood Family Rosary

My children, tonight, I bless each one of you. Do not have any doubt, but open your hearts to your heavenly Mother. I have much to teach you about love. I am here to help and protect you. I am so happy that you remain committed to praying the Rosary. You are all beautiful flowers that send the aroma of love to others through your prayer.

My children, I ask you to prepare through prayer when you gather together, for this is your time with me. (She did not want us to be visiting with each other. Tonight we were loud). Some of you have concerns about your family, and some of you are having problems in your marriages. Trust God with your problems and have faith.

I am Your Mother Come from Heaven to Love You

Message from Our Lady, February 8, 1990 (Continued)

My children, some of you have been suffering, for you are not in a prayerful spirit. Do not be distracted with this, but pray. Prepare for the Passion of my Son (she meant Lent), through the guidance of the Holy Spirit. The Holy Spirit will enlighten you and lead you through these forty days.

Tonight, I come to prepare your hearts to enter into a time of much prayer and fasting. Be receptive to my invitation.

One Year Anniversary, February 15, 1990

We had a family celebration with only a few friends. No message was given. Our Lady was here to bless us and to thank us for everything.

Message from Our Lady, February 22, 1990
Neighborhood Family Rosary

My children, tonight, I invite you to open your hearts totally to the Lord. Some of you are struggling with the spirit of doubt.

My children, I am here to help you, and I hold you close to my Immaculate Heart. Do not be afraid, but abandon yourselves with open hearts to God. Be strong and live in the light of truth.

My children, I am calling you to be my witnesses and to take my love to all your families. Pray and fast, my children; some of you have stopped fasting. Through prayer and fasting you obtain answers to your prayers. Do not become distracted with the world around you, but trust my Son and keep your eyes on Him, Who gave His life for love of you. Pray for the grace of obedience to do all that is required of you as children of God.

21

I am Your Mother Come from Heaven to Love You

Message from Our Lady, February 28, 1990
Neighborhood Family Rosary

My children, tonight, I bless you all. I invite you to pray for the gift of discernment to know the Will of God. I invite all the youth to be witnesses to other young people. Spread the Good News and bring others to my Son, Jesus. I bless you all, my children. Have no fear or doubt, but trust God. Offer up all your suffering in reparation for peace and conversion throughout the world.

Message from Our Lady, March 7,1990
Lent

My children, tonight, I invite you to live in total abandonment to God and to my Most Immaculate Heart. My children, I will teach you how to pray and fast. All I ask is that you open your hearts to my teachings.

Message from Jesus in the Blessed Sacrament
April 11, 1990, 10:50 a.m.

My dear child, I, your Jesus of Love and Mercy, thank you deeply with deep gratitude for all the suffering that you endured so lovingly and patiently. Know, My little flower, that many souls were redeemed through your long and painful suffering. Again, I thank you.

My little one, you have been united to My Cross and I am here to tell you that you endured all your suffering without complaining. You embraced your cross with great love for you were not thinking of your own pain. You were courageous in your suffering as you suffered for others. Every prayer that you prayed to the Father was received by My Father, and your prayers had the fragrance of brotherly love and love for all of mankind as you recommended the conversion of the whole world to My Father. Again, I thank you.

I am Your Mother Come from Heaven to Love You

Message from Jesus in the Blessed Sacrament
April 11, 1990 (Continued)

Janie
Jesus, I didn't make it to any of the Easter Celebration. How can I say you are welcome? My Jesus, my yes to you is a total yes from my heart and soul. I did only what was expected of me as a humble servant in my Father's Kingdom. Let me instead, give praise to the Almighty Father forever and ever for all the blessings that I have received throughout my life. To Him alone all glory be. Hosanna to God in the Highest, blessed be He that comes in the Name of the Lord. Hosanna in the Highest forever and ever. Amen. Alleluia.

Jesus
You have responded with your heart, and your praise of thanksgiving only continues to give glory to My Father. You are blessed, oh how you are blessed!

Now, My little one, I say to you, My peace I give you, My peace be with you. As My Father has sent Me, so I send you to go out and share this peace with all the places in the world that My Father calls you to. Forgive everyone and God will forgive you.

Now, I speak to all My children all over the world. As I appeared to all My disciples, so I come to you, to give you My peace and My love. I, your risen Jesus, ask that you love one another as I have loved you, share My peace and live in this peace. Take courage and live in faith, for I, your risen Jesus, have overcome the world. Live together and pray together, harvesting the Kingdom of My Father.

To My beloved priests, to you I say have faith and do not be the doubting Thomas who had to see Me to believe that I had risen. I am with each one of you my beloved brothers, and to you I ask, do you love Me? Then feed my lambs, and take care of My sheep and be ready to suffer for them and with them. Open your hearts and be prepared to attend and guide the flock entrusted into your care.

My beloved brothers, pick up your cross every day and follow Me, your Jesus and your brother. As I appeared to all My disciples, My beloved priests, I am with you each day in the celebration of Holy Mass. Be made pure and allow yourselves to be transformed by My Precious Blood.

I am Your Mother Come from Heaven to Love You

Message from Jesus in the Blessed Sacrament
April 11, 1990 (Continued)

Many of you have abandoned Me as Simon Peter did. To you, I, your Master say, come back to Me and I will make you whole. In Me you will be healed from all your woundedness. Do not be afraid of anything around you, not your suffering nor your persecution; fear nothing. I, your Jesus of Mercy, hold you, all My beloved, in the palm of My hand. Your names are inscribed in My Heart. I am with each one of you, My beloved, until the end of time. Live in harmony, in love, in peace. Bring unity to My Body. I love you, My beloved. Be obedient, be made pure through this love of Mine.

To all families in the world, to you, I, your Jesus say, live in My love and My peace, loving one another. Live and put into practice My Father's Ten Commandments and teach your children all that I am teaching you. Live as a holy family. Pray together, grow together, share God's blessings with others. Fear nothing around you, but prepare your hearts and work together in My Father's Kingdom, harvesting and cultivating one another's hearts through your prayers and sacrifices.

Now, I give My blessings to all the world, and as I bless you, know that special blessings and graces are being poured out upon the Church and to all souls all over the world. This special blessing will help you in your walk with Me, your risen Christ.

My peace I give to you, not as the world gives, but as I, your Jesus of Love and Mercy give. I love you all My beloved ones. Peace, peace, peace!

Janie
Thank you my Jesus, thank you!

Jesus
You are most welcome.

Janie
I love you.

I am Your Mother Come from Heaven to Love You

Message from Our Lord Jesus, April 23, 1990
During my illness

My child, offer all your suffering for your family's conversion and for all who are distant from My heart.

Message from Our Lord Jesus in the Blessed Sacrament
April 24, 1990

I was asking Jesus how I could serve Him without failing. I felt that I wasn't doing enough, praying enough. I was having problems with anger and in being patient with others at work and at home. Jesus spoke these words:

"My child, do not be concerned with small details. It pleases Me that you are aware of your shortcomings with others. The fact that you worry about displeasing Me demonstrates your love for Me.

As you abandon yourself totally to Me, the evil one will attempt to bring more difficulties your way. I ask that you trust Me in everything. Keep your heart united with Mine."

Message from Our Lady, April 25, 1990
Message to my family

My children, you please your heavenly Mother that you are trying hard to draw closer to my Son and to please Him. Through my intercession and teachings you are coming to know my Son more and more.

When you fast as a family, offer your prayers and fasting for all my beloved priests and for the Holy Souls in Purgatory. Pray for world peace and trust in my Immaculate Heart.

25

I am Your Mother Come from Heaven to Love You

Message from Our Lord Jesus
While I was praying, April 25, 1990

My child, do not be afraid when you are being distracted by Satan and all his lies. Remember, he is the father of lies, and he will tell you lies to destroy you. He will work on your weak points to discourage you.

My child, remember, you and your family are the sons and daughters of the Eternal Father, therefore, you are children of the light. Through My Death and Resurrection you received My power and authority to defend yourself through prayer when the evil one attacks you with his lies.

My child, meditate on these Scriptures: Luke 10: 1-12 and Luke 10: 17-20. Remember that your name and many others who live as children of the light - these souls' names are written in the Book of Life. Allow faith and love to be your strength.

Message from Our Lord Jesus in the Blessed Sacrament
April 25, 1990

I was sad over some family matters, and I was hurting in my heart. Jesus spoke these words to me:

"My child, you are upset that your family is much occupied with television. Pray for them. It hurts Me also, when My children don't think about Me."

I asked, "What can I do?"

Jesus responded, "Offer this suffering for your own conversion and for theirs as well. Conversion is a process, and much prayer is needed to nurture the soul. Tomorrow, My child, fast on bread and water. It will be difficult for you, for the evil one will be strong in distracting you. As you suffer, your loved ones will draw closer to Me. Prepare well in the morning through prayer, and meditate on this Scripture, John 20: 24-29."

I am Your Mother Come from Heaven to Love You

Message from Our Lord Jesus, April 26, 1990

Today, I had family problems. I was upset because my relatives never visit me or act like my family. I was telling Jesus all this when I asked Him, "Jesus, during Your Passion and all during Your ministry, when You were healing and performing all Your miracles and people were mistreating You, did You feel like You wanted to stop doing everything for our sake?"

Jesus answered: "No, My child, for love never gives up. I understand your deep pain. My child, you are experiencing some of My painful Passion of rejection. My own people rejected Me and called Me 'mad.' They uttered unpleasant things about Me, but I loved them even more, and you must love them too, even in your deepest suffering. Through your suffering conversion will be born in their hearts."

Message from Our Lady, April 30, 1990
Family Rosary - Holy Hour

While we were praying our family Rosary, during the third Mystery Our Lady was with us. She had Baby Jesus in her arms. She spoke these words:

"My children, tonight I come with the Child Jesus." (She extended her arms and handed Jesus to us). "Take Him; He is the gift of love to the world. Accept His love and be converted."

I am Your Mother Come from Heaven to Love You

Message from Our Lady, May 3, 1990
Family Rosary - Holy Hour

Tonight, Our Lord and Our Lady were very present during the Rosary. Many family members came to pray with us. Tonight marks one year of Holy Hour prayer, of praying the Rosary. My family smelled sweet roses and myrrh for the first time. Our Lady spoke these words:

"My child, remember when I first called you and charged you and your family with praying the Rosary and leading others to prayer?"

I responded, "Yes, my Lady."

"Listen, my child to how beautiful they sound as they pray their Rosary and how strong their prayer is."

I looked at my family. They looked beautiful. I have heard angels praying, but my family sounded beautiful.

Our Lady then gave this message: "My children, pray, pray, for only in this way will your hearts be converted!"

Message from Our Lady while visiting the Blessed Sacrament
May 4, 1990

Our Lady
My child, tomorrow, many of my children will come to honor me and my heart is joyful. (She was referring to the May Crowning).

Janie
My Lady, Sister wants me to give a speech about the Rosary and devotion to you. Should I write down anything?

Our Lady
I will speak to your heart, and these are my words: My little children, I, your heavenly Mother, love you all. I invite you to return back to the sacraments and to pray for one another. Live the Gospel, my children, and pray your Rosary every day.

28

I am Your Mother Come from Heaven to Love You

Message from Our Lord Jesus and Our Lady
At the Blessed Sacrament, May 6, 1990

Jesus
My child, you have been making reparation and cultivating souls and talking to many about My Kingdom. This pleases Me. You are concerned about the salvation of others, and you are generous in your prayers for others. You, My child, spend much time praying for the needs of the entire world. You cover every area of the world as the Holy Spirit enlightens you. Continue praying and making reparation for the needs of the world. Bring Me all your concerns, and I will attend to them.

Janie
My adorable Jesus, teach me how to suffer and give me this grace. I don't know how to accept my suffering and my crosses in my daily walk with You. Please Jesus, teach me.

Jesus reassured me that He would help me.

Our Lady
My dear child, how much you please your heavenly Mother by asking my Son for the grace to suffer. Do not be concerned; my Son and I will teach you. God is pleased with your work and all your dedication in bringing others to my Son.

I am Your Mother Come from Heaven to Love You

Message from Our Lord Jesus in the Blessed Sacrament
Before Mass, May 10, 1990

Jesus

My child, thank you for coming and for greeting Me as Your Adorable Savior. This title is pleasing to Me. Leave Me all your concerns. I don't want you to have any worries, only trust Me and love Me.

Janie

During Mass, I had a vision of a road and a vision of the Eucharist. Later, I asked Jesus to explain it to me. I saw a road going from one heart to another heart.

Jesus

My child, the road that you saw is the road that leads to Heaven.

Janie

Adorable Savior, please explain the two hearts.

Jesus

My child, the heart coming from below was your heart. The road is the path to Heaven; and the other heart that was in the Heavens was My Father's heart. The vision of the Eucharist along the road: that is Me. I am The Way to the Father. Only through repentance and eating of My Body and drinking My Blood will redemption take place in sinful hearts. Share this with others, as it is important that they learn about salvation through attending daily Mass and feeding on the Holy Eucharist as their daily food.

Message from Our Lady, May 11, 1990
Family Rosary - Holy Hour

My dear children, tonight, I invite you to pray with open hearts. Be converted, be converted! Again I say, open your hearts, for I cannot help you if your hearts are closed!

Pray for conversion, before it's too late! Please, dear children, help me, help me by trusting in my motherly intercession. Peace must reign in your hearts!

I am Your Mother Come from Heaven to Love You

Message from Our Lord Jesus, May 12, 1990
Concerning Fear

My child, do not be afraid, but pray. Prayer brings you to perfection and to peace. When fear fills your heart, drive fear out through praying. Know that I, your Jesus, am with you.

Message from Our Lady, May 26, 1990
Family Rosary - Holy Hour

My dear children, pray unceasingly, for prayer is your strength and prayer brings you peace.

Message from Our Lord Jesus in the Blessed Sacrament
May 27, 1990

I was praying to Jesus to help me, for my heart felt dry.

Jesus spoke these words to me: "My dear child, whenever you experience dry spells in your heart, it is not because I am not with you, for I will never abandon you. These dry spells help you to grow in faith. You see, My child, once the soul comes to know Me, that soul suffers when it feels abandoned by Me. It is during this time that I am the strongest, for when you are weak then I become strong in you. Your suffering also helps you to become stronger in prayer and in trusting in Me, your Source of eternal life."

I am Your Mother Come from Heaven to Love You

Message from Our Lord Jesus in the Blessed Sacrament
Later this day, May 27, 1990

My child, pray for My beloved brothers (the priests), for they are becoming fewer and fewer in numbers. Make reparation for their suffering and persecutions, for there is much suffering among My brothers. I love them so, I love them so. Pray for them.

Message from Our Lady, May 28, 1990
Family Rosary - Holy Hour

Tonight, Our Lady told me that I would go to Medjugorje, although she knew I had a fear of flying. Her message was given in Blanco, Texas. My family and I were visiting there.

Dear children, pray unceasingly! If you only understood the importance of prayer, you would pray with love in your hearts. Pray together as a family, attend Mass together, visit my Son often. There is so much suffering in the world because of lack of prayer. Please do not close your hearts, for when you stop praying my Immaculate and Sorrowful Heart suffers for you. I cannot help you if you do not pray. Pray, pray, pray!

Message from Our Lady, June 5, 1990

I was having problems and struggles with my family. Our Lady spoke these words to me:

"My dear child, have no concern in your heart, for you have been helping your family draw closer to my Son. You have taught your family the importance of prayer. Your own prayers have helped you to grow in wisdom and discernment. You have brought joy to your Mother's heart.

I am Your Mother Come from Heaven to Love You

Message from Our Lady, June 5, 1990 (Continued)

My child, know that when you take care of your family out of love and obedience, you are also at prayer. (Sometimes I got irritated when I had to stop praying to attend to my family. No one knew this except Jesus and Mary). This, my child, pleases God.

My little one, you have been trying so very hard to be obedient in doing all that is asked of you as a wife and mother. You are growing in the virtue of obedience as well. Remember, obedience is a first class virtue. You obtain sanctity and purity through obedience."

Message from Our Lady later this day, June 5, 1990
Family Rosary - Holy Hour

Dear children, tonight, I invite you to continue to pray. My children, you are so beautiful when you are in prayer. The fragrance of your prayer pleases me so, for it is prayer of the heart. Continue to pray your Rosary.

Dear children, know that I am with you when you are in prayer. You have prayed so beautifully as a family. You have made me very happy.

Know, my little ones, that I am always interceding for you and asking God to bless you. Continue to pray as a family, and you will receive blessings, blessings, blessings!

I am Your Mother Come from Heaven to Love You

Message from Jesus in the Blessed Sacrament and Our Lady
June 11, 1990

Janie
Greetings, my beloved Savior. I came to visit with You. What can I do
for You?

Jesus
My child, welcome to My Eucharistic Heart and thank you for coming
to spend time with Me.

My little one, you ask Me what you can do for Me. I, your Jesus, ask
you to take Me to your family and to others and share My love with
them. Tell them all how much I love them. Invite them to come and
visit with Me. I will give them joy and peace. I will heal their wounded
hearts. In Me they will find rest, and I will relieve them of their
burdens, for I am gentle of Heart and My yoke is light. I desire that
you do this for Me, and that you continue your visits with Me, your
beloved Savior.

Janie
What can I do for you, my Lady?

Our Lady
My daughter, my desire is the same as my Son. I, too, ask that you
take me to share my love with others. Tell my children how much I
love them. I desire that you come and visit with my Son, everyday.
Through these visits you will learn much about Our love for you. Your
faith will grow and little by little you will believe that God has found
favor in you.

Janie
I do believe in what you say my Lady, and I want to come to visit your
Son, but I don't know my schedule. Please give me the grace I need
to be obedient to your request.

Our Lady
My child, your request will be granted because of your honest heart.
Go in my Son's peace.

I am Your Mother Come from Heaven to Love You

Message from Our Lady, June 21, 1990
Family Rosary - Holy Hour

My dear children, tonight, I invite you to be witnesses of the Gospel and to live in God's peace. I invite you to read Holy Scripture every day, and God will bless you. God will bless you!

Message from Our Lord Jesus in the Blessed Sacrament
While on retreat, July 24, 1990

I went on a retreat out of town with two friends and a priest. This was a very special time, as these two friends were receiving visitations from Our Lady. It was Our Lady's request that I go and stay with them for five days.

My child, I brought you here to give you a special blessing through My son, the priest. Know, My child, that your suffering will come through many of My beloved brother priests. They will reject everything you have been receiving on teachings of the family.

Your bishop will come to know about you when the time comes for you to be known. Your messages will be made public.

My child, you will suffer when My brother priests reject you as they reject Me. Remain calm through all this when the time comes, for you will endure all the suffering and rejection.

Your own family members (distant relatives) will doubt, and some of your friends will become jealous of all the blessings and wisdom that you receive.

Do not fear, My child, for just as many of My brother priests reject you, many of My other brother priests will believe in what you are receiving to be divine. These are My brother priests whose hearts are open to My Mother's Immaculate Heart. These are My brother priests that love My Mother.

I am Your Mother Come from Heaven to Love You

Message from Our Lord Jesus in the Blessed Sacrament
July 24, 1990 (Continued)

Many of My brother priests will come to you for advice and prayers. Do not worry when this time comes, for the Holy Spirit will enlighten you on what to say. Many of My brother priests will love and respect you. They will help you and defend you.

Remember, My child, My special blessing will help you in times of persecution from the Church. Keep your eyes on Me, and you will embrace all your persecution with joy.

Message from Our Lady, July 25, 1990

Dear children, do not be afraid during trials and sufferings. Pray and have an open heart. There is much suffering within the family, and the suffering will increase. Pray for those who are having a hard time converting. Reach out to them with love. Pray for all who are suffering. Take my Son to all who you meet and tell them how my Son loves them. Pray your Rosary with your family and be converted!

Message from Our Lord Jesus in the Blessed Sacrament
July 26, 1990

My child, never allow anyone or anything to separate you from My love. Do not allow pride to distract you from My love. Trust Me in everything and never take your eyes off of Me, your Jesus of Love and Mercy.

I am Your Mother Come from Heaven to Love You

Prayer inspired by the Holy Spirit, July 27, 1990
Feast of the Precious Blood

CONSECRATION TO THE PRECIOUS BLOOD

Dear Jesus, I thank you for all you have done for me.

Take me, Jesus. I offer myself to you all over again. Let me remain with you forever. Make me an instrument of your peace.

Teach me obedience, so that I may do God's Will. Give me an open heart, that I may always be at prayer.

Touch my mind Jesus, bless me with the gift of comprehension, so that I may always understand what you teach me.

Bless and touch my eyes that I may only see you, my ears that I may only hear your words, my nose that I may always smell the fragrance of your Divine Will, my mouth that all I say be pure and holy.

Bless my hands so I may help others, my feet that I may walk towards the path of holiness. Amen.

I am Your Mother Come from Heaven to Love You

Message from Our Lord Jesus in the Blessed Sacrament
Retreat, July 28, 1990

My child, I want to thank you for coming to spend time with Me. My child, I know that it was hard for you to leave your family. Do not worry about your family, I am with them as I am also with you. Trust Me while you are here and allow the Holy Spirit to enlighten your heart.

During your retreat I will speak to you of many things, and you will hold all that I tell you dear to your heart. My Mother will help you in the areas that you need her assistance. Be at peace My child, be at peace while you are away from your family.

My child, take My love to your family and share with them everything I tell you, for it will help them too.

Message from Our Lady, July 28, 1990
Retreat

My sweet angel, do all that my Son commands you to do. Know, my child, that my Son and I will help you in everything. Be open to Our teaching and guidance while you are here.

Message from Our Lady, August 15, 1990
Feast of the Assumption

Dear children, you have brought me much joy through your love in honoring me on this my feast day. Know, my dear children, that when you come together for prayer, your prayers are answered.

I am Your Mother Come from Heaven to Love You

Message from Our Lord Jesus, August 19, 1990

My Dear Child,

It was I, your Jesus of Love and Mercy, who called you to come and spend time with Me, for I know that you are suffering.

My child, you have many thoughts running through your mind. Satan is trying hard to over power your mind, but he cannot do it! You belong to Me!

You have received blessings and graces through your prayers. Never forget this. You are protected, and you protect your family through your prayers.

I know, My child, that you feel sad when you cannot attend Mass. I know how much it hurts you when your family does not want to join you in prayer. Continue to pray for your family. Offer all your suffering for their and all other families' conversions.

Know, My child, that right this minute I have given your family peace, through your intercession for them. Love your family as I love you. Be patient with them and entrust them to Me, your Jesus of Love and Mercy.

Message from Our Lady, August 19, 1990

My precious angel, do not be concerned about your family, but do as my Son tells you and offer your suffering for your family and for peace in the world.

Remember, my precious child, take refuge in the Sacred Heart of my Son and my Most Immaculate Heart, for in the Two United Hearts lies your protection.

Return to your prayers and do not worry about your family. They, too, are under Our protection.

I am Your Mother Come from Heaven to Love You

Message from Our Lady, August 21, 1990

<u>Janie</u>
Dear Lady, I am concerned about this trip. Are you really calling me to go to Medjugorje?

<u>Our Lady</u>
I am inviting you to go and visit this holy area. When you go you will experience a tremendous amount of grace like never before. I have chosen this place for the conversion of many. Do not be concerned about this trip, but trust in my intercession and continue to pray.

<u>Janie</u>
Will my visitation with you come to an end? Is this why you are calling me to go visit this place?

<u>Our Lady</u>
The day will come when I will no longer visit with you in the way that I am doing now.

<u>Janie</u>
Blessed Mother, please don't tell me just now. I can't take it. (I began to cry).

<u>Our Lady</u>
Be strong, my angel, for I will always be with you, especially in times of difficulties. You will know that I am with you. On your birthday, I will be with you in a special way. You will feel my presence on special feast days.

I am Your Mother Come from Heaven to Love You

Message from Our Lady, August 23, 1990

I had been sad since Our Lady had told me that the day would come when she would stop visiting me. This never occurred to me since I knew nothing of Mary and that such visits could take place. I had asked Jesus to let me suffer and to let me feel my sadness for my own conversion.

Our Lady said, "My dear angel, I know that you are very sad and it saddens my Immaculate Heart to see you so sad. My child, I will never abandon you. I will always live in your heart. Please allow your heavenly Mother to console you. Do not shut me out, I love you my precious angel, I love you. Let me help you in your sorrow."

I prayed with her and suddenly my heart was full of joy. I knew that she would always love me and be with me. I knew this, oh, how I knew it in my heart. I was so thankful to God for Our Lady's love for all her children.

Message from Our Lord Jesus in the Blessed Sacrament
August 23, 1990

Dear Child,

I, your Jesus, thank you for coming to spend time with Me.

My precious one, I know that you are sad and that you are suffering. Offer all your suffering and pain for the poor souls that are having a difficult time converting.

Pray and fast for these souls whom Satan keeps in bondage through their sins. (He meant that these souls refuse to be reconciled back to God, therefore, they remain in sin).

Pray and be strong in your suffering. Remember, I am always with you. I will never abandon you. Remember all the blessings that My heavenly Father has blessed you with. Cling to these blessings. Be at peace, My child.

I am Your Mother Come from Heaven to Love You

Message from Our Lady, August 23, 1990
Family Holy Hour

Dear children, you bring joy to my heart when you pray together as a family. Pray, dear children, for many souls are going astray. They live in darkness because of lack of prayer.

Pray and fast, for through prayer and fasting many who want to convert are able to do so.

My children, I am here to help you, for I know that there is much suffering in your families. Do not be afraid when you look at your situation, rather rejoice and offer everything to God Who knows your hearts.

Know that I love you all dearly, and your refuge is my Most Immaculate Heart. I invite you, dear children, to help your heavenly Mother with your prayers. Be reconciled back to God and be converted! Time is short! Pray, children, and be converted, be converted!

I am Your Mother Come from Heaven to Love You

A Messenger from Heaven, September 10, 1990

I received this visit while I was in prayer. I had been struggling with believing if all my visitations were of divine origin. Although my spiritual director said the visits were divine, I still struggled. I believe this was the reason for this visit.

She greeted me and said Our Lady had sent her to talk with me and to help me. She wore a dazzling white dress and had flowers in her hair. Then the messenger began speaking to me.

These are her words: "As you know, Most Holy Mary has been appearing to six children in Medjugorje and has been teaching the world through them. You have also been chosen by God and you must be obedient to doing the Will of God. The Queen of Heaven has come to you and your family to teach you about family love. You must do all that she tells you.

(I thought to myself, nobody will believe this).

It is not important that anyone else believes, but that you yourself believe in your heart. You have been given a mission, a mission of cultivating the hearts of the families through your prayers and sacrifices. Much responsibility has been entrusted to you, and you must be obedient and trust God with this mission.

You must never grow tired of doing what Most Holy Mary is asking of you. Your faith is your strength, and you must live with the kind of faith that only exists in Heaven.

(I guess she means to pray for strong faith, so that I may accomplish all that God is calling me to accomplish).

Live Heaven on earth, doing only holy deeds. Serve God in all that you do. Love everyone always.

(I had lost a Rosary, so I asked her if she would ask Our Lady about my Rosary).

Most Holy Mary will help you to find your Rosary. Remember, do everything that Most Holy Mary is asking of you. Offer all your prayers and sacrifices with love. Love God in everything. Farewell, my friend, farewell. Remember my words!"

43

I am Your Mother Come from Heaven to Love You

Message from Our Lady, September 10, 1990
Later that same day

My angel, do not be concerned about this visit, but believe with your heart. My angel, Heaven has chosen you. You have been entrusted with much responsibility. You will help to bring many families to God through your prayers and sacrifices.

Do not be concerned about the trip to Medjugorje. I am preparing everything for you and your husband.

<u>Janie</u>
My Lady, I am sorry for not finishing all my prayers.

<u>Our Lady</u>
Do not be concerned. I know you will get all your prayers prayed. I must go, my angel, be at peace.

Message from Our Lady, September 13, 1990
Family Rosary - Holy Hour

My children, I, your heavenly Mother, invite you to continue to pray as a family. Know, my little ones, that Satan is active, trying to destroy you.

Love one another and know that through your love you will obtain many blessings from God.

My children, I turn to you to console your heavenly Mother through your prayers. Pray for all my children throughout the world. Love one another, love one another.

I am Your Mother Come from Heaven to Love You

Message from Our Lady, October 5, 1990

<u>Our Lady</u>
My dear angel, why do you worry so, and suffer in vain?

<u>Janie</u>
Please, dear Lady, what do you mean, suffer in vain?

<u>Our Lady</u>
My dear one, you suffer needlessly. It is the evil one who puts all these thoughts in your mind about me.

My angel, I have been with you for almost two years now, and I will remain with you a short while longer after you make your trip to Medjugorje. I want you to use this time wisely and to come to me whenever you need to. Bring me all your concerns, for I have come to help you and teach you about my Son and His love and mercy.

Do not be sad because I told you that my time is short, but be happy and show your gratitude to God for allowing me to be with you and your family. Share my Son's love with everyone you meet, especially with your family.

I am Your Mother Come from Heaven to Love You

Message from Our Lady, October 13, 1990

I had awakened from a most disturbing dream, and I asked Our Lady to come and explain this dream to me. In my dream I had seen violence, fighting, bombing, buildings being destroyed, people getting hurt, and some were killed.

Janie
My Lady, could you please explain my dream; it was very frightening. Is there going to be a war?

Our Lady
Yes, my angel, a war will break out soon. Fear will come among many. The economy will suffer where this war breaks out. Many will be homeless and they will have no jobs. Many innocent victims will be wounded, and others will die.

Janie
Am I to share this?

Our Lady
Yes, for much prayer will be needed to bring this war to an end. Its duration will be short, but many will suffer. Share this with your spiritual director right away, so that he will begin to offer the Holy Mass and prayers for this intention.

Many will begin to pray again during this time. The churches will be filled, for many will be praying for their loved ones.

Janie
Blessed Mother, what if my spiritual director doesn't believe me?

Our Lady
My dear angel, just do as I ask you. Your spiritual director will believe you, for I have prepared his heart for this time. Call him and share this message with him.

Message from Our Lady, October 13, 1990 (Continued)

I was afraid to call my spiritual director and share this message, because I didn't know how he would react. I prayed to the Holy Spirit to help me, then I called him.

He believed me right away and agreed to do what Our Lady asked him to do. He even thanked me for being obedient to Our Lady and sharing this message with him.

Message from Our Lord Jesus, October 20, 1990

My little flower, pray and fast in reparation for the sins of the world. Through prayer and fasting you obtain answers to your prayers. Share this with others.

Message from Our Lady, October 22, 1990

My dear angel, thank you for being obedient in doing all that I am asking of you. God will bless you, God will bless you! Know that I am with you always.

I am Your Mother Come from Heaven to Love You

Message from Our Lady, November 1, 1990
Dallas, Texas

My dear angel, I invite you and your family to begin forming prayer Cenacles in your community. Go to your priest and ask his blessing in this effort. Share this with your spiritual director and get his approval first.

The Holy Spirit will enlighten you as you help other families to begin praying together in their homes. As the family Cenacles grow, then you can begin to move to the Church.

In this way, all families can join together. Blessings will come upon those who respond to my invitation. Later, you will help guide the youth to form Cenacles and pray the Rosary. God will bless all your prayers and efforts, and through your family's prayers God will bless many families. Much conversion in the family will be the fruits of your obedience.

Message from Our Lady, November 29, 1990

Our Lady
My child, I invite you to be a witness of living my messages when you return to your home in America. Commit to coming together once a week and praying the Rosary with my children who have joined you in this journey.

Share my messages with all people you meet. I have brought you here to bless you in a special way, to help you in the work that you will do in the future.

Janie
My dear Lady, I will do as you ask, and I will live your messages. I will pray for my own conversion and for the conversion of the world. I will start a Rosary group, and we will meet once a week.

I am Your Mother Come from Heaven to Love You

Message from Our Lady, February 19, 1991

FIRST MESSAGE FROM OUR LADY TO THE PRAYER GROUP

Dear children, do not be afraid, but go forth and serve God with joy. Be strong my children, be strong and do not fear. Be loving, my children, and let love be your strength. Thank you for listening to my message.

Message from Our Lady, February 28, 1991

SECOND MESSAGE FROM OUR LADY TO THE PRAYER GROUP

Dear children, you are so dear to me, and I thank you for coming together for prayer. Through your prayer you will draw closer to my Son.

You will grow through prayer.

Know, my children, that as you come together for prayer, I, your heavenly Mother, will be with you. I will teach you about love and prayer in your family. I will guide you in your prayers. I will teach you prayer of the heart.

My children, I will help you to live my messages and to share my messages with your family. I ask, little children, that you prepare your hearts for my motherly teaching and guidance. Thank you for listening to my message.

I am Your Mother Come from Heaven to Love You

Message from Our Lady, March 7, 1991

Dear children, love and peace. I thank you for all of your hard work in living my messages and sharing them with others.

Today, I invite you to be a loving family and to forgive one another. Only through love and forgiveness will you achieve peace in your family.

Learn to forgive from the heart. Abandon all grudges and you will obtain God's peace. Thank you for listening to my message.

Message from Our Lady, March 12, 1991

Dear children, I bring you my motherly love, and I ask you to trust in my intercession. Be loving to one another and do not allow anything to keep you from doing God's Will. My children, I am praying with you and for you. Thank you for listening to my message.

Message from Our Lady, March 18, 1991

Dear children, today, I invite you to live in God's peace and to extend His peace to others. My children, learn to love with your hearts and be at peace with one another. Pray together as a family and know that I am praying with you when you gather for family prayer. Thank you for listening to my message.

I am Your Mother Come from Heaven to Love You

Message from Our Lady, March 28, 1991

Dear children, today, I invite you to continue to pray and to trust God with all your prayers. Do not be discouraged in your suffering, but endure your crosses with joy. Abandon yourselves to my Immaculate Heart and allow me to help you to be pure and holy.

Pray and fast, my children, and decide for conversion. Live my messages and pray, pray, pray! Thank you for listening to my message.

Message from Our Lady, April 2, 1991

Dear children, know that I love you very much. I have come from Heaven to help you to know and love my Son. I am with you each step of the way. Pray, children, pray! Thank you for listening to my message.

Message from Our Lady, April 16, 1991, 10:30 a.m.

Dear children, love and pray for one another. You know, dear children, that I have come to love and help you. Pray, and pray very hard for time is running out. You, dear children, must pray so that all souls will be converted, especially those most distant from my Son's Heart.

Message from Our Lady, April 22, 1991, 12:00 p.m.

Dear children, my heart is so sad, because so many of my children have stopped praying. Please, dear children, I need your help.

Pray, dear children, pray, for there is so much suffering in this world. Be converted, dear children, be converted!

I am Your Mother Come from Heaven to Love You

Message from Our Lady, April 29, 1991

Dear children, thank you for all the work and prayers that you are doing. Dear children, pray and do not be afraid. Believe in the love that my Son has for you and continue in your prayers and in loving one another.

Pray your Rosaries every day, dear children, and pray with your hearts, pray with your hearts.

Message from Jesus, May 9, 1991
Ascension Thursday

My Brothers and Sisters,

I have ascended that you may have eternal life. Love and pray for one another and listen to My Mother.

My brothers and sisters, I have come, because I am pleased with these prayer gatherings. My Mother and I are pleased with these prayer gatherings. My Mother and I are pleased to be here on this special day.

Pray always to the Holy Spirit, because when you pray to the Holy Spirit, you speak directly to My Father's heart.

Message from Our Lady, May 9, 1991, later the same day.

Dear children, know that I am with you. I have come to take you to Heaven with me. Dear children, I am here to help you to be clean.

Please, dear children, help me. Let your prayer be prayer of the heart, where you will find peace and love. Live my messages, dear children, and take my messages seriously. Live my messages every day!

I am Your Mother Come from Heaven to Love You

Message from Our Lady, May 22, 1991,11:30 a.m.

Dear children, pray and trust, dear children, pray and trust. You, dear children, do not know how to open your hearts to the Holy Spirit. Do not be afraid, for I am here to help you. Prayer is the answer to all your suffering. Learn to pray, dear children, and allow your hearts to open up in prayer. Take refuge in my Immaculate Heart and be converted from the heart.

Dear children, I love you and I am here to help you. Trust, dear children, trust and pray, and suffer for the love of others.

Pray the Rosary, pray the Rosary, pray the Rosary!

Message from Our Lady, May 28, 1991, 11:40 a.m.

Dear children, I am here to take you to Heaven with me. You, dear children, must pray so that you can have a pure heart. Do not be afraid, dear children, but be converted!

Dear children, you are so precious to the Lord. If you only knew how great the love of God is for you. Please, dear children, pray! Pray all the time! Find time for prayer, for through your prayer many souls can be converted.

Time is running out, dear children, so be obedient and pray, fast, and be converted, be converted! Peace, dear children, peace. I love you, dear children. I desire that peace will reign in all my children.

I desire, dear children, that you pray the complete Rosary. Pray for love, peace, conversion within the Church. Pray for your families, yourselves, and do not forget the Poor Souls in Purgatory or the unborn.

I am Your Mother Come from Heaven to Love You

Message from Jesus, May 28, 1991, 11:40 a.m.

Jesus came to visit. From His Heart were shining colors of red and golden yellow, and there were brilliant flames. The light from His Heart was indescribable.

Jesus said, "This is My Love and Mercy. Take it, take it unto others. Obey My Mother. Love and honor her. Look at My Sacred Heart. It bleeds for all the sinfulness of this world. Come and take refuge in My Sacred Heart."

Message from Our Lady, May 28, 1991, later that same day.

My dear children, my heart is so joyful, because through your obedience some of my children are returning back to my Son. Your prayers and your offerings are so important. Please, I beg you dear children, pray, pray, pray!

Message from Our Lady, June 25, 1991

Dear children, pray as a family, for Satan is so active, and he wants to destroy you. Pray, dear children, pray and be strong. Do not be afraid of anything, but pray!

I am Your Mother Come from Heaven to Love You

Message from Our Lady, July 10, 1991

My Child,

Today, I, your heavenly Mother, ask that you join your prayers to mine. Open your heart to what I am about to tell you concerning the world. Write what I tell you.

My heart is pierced with sadness, for my children continue to ignore my messages. They continue to live in sin, and in doing this they lead others to sin. If my children continue to ignore my messages, much suffering will take place, and many innocent victims will suffer and die because of hard and obstinate hearts.

A war has begun in Yugoslavia. This situation will get worse. Many will suffer and die. Many will be left homeless. Innocent families will suffer. I ask much prayer of all my children for this war.

There will be wars in different parts of the world where many will die. Earthquakes will destroy many souls. Drought will destroy crops, and my children who are farmers will suffer immensely. There will be much famine, and all these disasters will cause the economy to suffer. Some of these disasters are taking place now, but it will become much worse.

The Church will suffer more and more. Priests will leave the priesthood. Many of my priests will go against the teaching of my Son's Vicar on earth. Division will grow more and more through lack of obedience. My beloved Pope will suffer in a physical way.

Much prayer is needed for my priests who continue to live in a time of great apostasy. Many do not acknowledge the true meaning of my Son's True Presence in the Most Holy Eucharist. This pierces my heart.

The family will suffer from violence, child abuse, rebellious sons and daughters, and the divorce rate will increase. Love and prayer will not be in existence in homes. Much division will separate the family.

Message from Our Lady, July 10, 1991 (Continued)

The youth will turn against their parents, many causing violence to their parents even to the point of killing their parents. Drug abuse will take many lives. Abortion will increase tremendously among the youth. They will bring fear to those around them, and they will cause much destruction to society.

My child, if my children do not listen and live my messages, it will be too late for them. Pray and fast, so that many will decide for conversion. The whole world is in need of much conversion, but I am deeply concerned about your country whose sins keep increasing with each moment that goes by.

My child, it is for the sake of all my children that I have remained in this world for so long. If my children do not pray, I cannot help them. If they do not pray, they cannot come to know God. It is only through prayer and fasting that conversion will take place.

Soon, my time in the world will come to an end. Pray, my child, pray, so that hearts will be converted before it's too late.

Message from Our Lady, July 22, 1991

Dear children, pray your Rosaries and return back to the sacraments, before it's too late! Pray with your hearts, dear children, and trust in your prayer. Love one another and pray for one another.

I am Your Mother Come from Heaven to Love You

Message from Our Lady, August,1, 1991

Dear children, pray and fast, pray and fast. Be reconciled and be converted!

Dear children, I come as the Queen of Peace. Therefore, I ask you to live in peace and to practice peace.

Do not be afraid to ask me for help. Many of you do not ask me for help, because you do not believe I am here. Open your hearts, for I only wish to lead you to Heaven.

Message from Our Lady, August 6, 1991

Dear children, know the importance of family prayer. Love one another. Again, I say, love one another. My heart is sad, little children, because there is no love in the family.

Be converted, be converted! I love you all, little children, and I am here to help you. Love one another and pray together as a family.

Little children, I have given this message many times. Know that if it was not important, I would not insist that you pray as a family.

Message from Our Lady, August 15, 1991
Feast of the Assumption

Dear children, rejoice and thank your heavenly Father for allowing me to come down from Heaven to help and guide you in your way to holiness.

Dear children, please trust in my intercession, for I am your heavenly Mother who loves you. Pray, dear children, and be converted. Only through prayer and conversion will you be able to attain pure hearts.

I am Your Mother Come from Heaven to Love You

Message from Our Lady, August 22, 1991
Queenship of Mary

Dear children, I am calling you to holiness. Do not be afraid, for nothing can harm you. Love one another and live the joy that God has placed in your hearts. Do not be afraid, my little ones, for I am with you each step of the way. You have much to learn, little children.

Message from Our Lady, September 2, 1991

Dear children, pray for obedience. For you, dear children, do not know how to be obedient. God has granted me this time to be with you.

Dear children, the conversion of the world is so important. I am depending on each one of you to do what God requires of you. My time is short, so please listen to me dear children, listen to me and be converted. Pray and fast!

Message from Our Lady, September 12, 1991

Dear children, today is a day of great rejoicing! Prepare your hearts through prayer and fasting, so that you may be able to do God's Will.

Dear children, you are so special to my heart, and I pray so for all my children. Rejoice, and live as children of the light. I am your heavenly Mother, and I have come to bring peace back into this world that continues to walk in darkness.

Dear children, please listen to all my messages and live them for each one is of great importance. Please believe in my messages and now, I say, peace, little children, peace.

I am Your Mother Come from Heaven to Love You

Message from Our Lady, September 17, 1991

Dear children, pray your Rosaries from the heart, for these are very important times. Pray with your families and love one another.

Dear children, do not get tired of serving God. Come, rather, and put all your trust in Him and decide for Him. When you fast, dear children, offer it for all the unbelievers who are walking in darkness.

Message from Our Lady, September 22, 1991, 11:30 a.m.

Dear children, how pleased you've made me with all your prayers and offerings. Heaven is rejoicing. Heaven is rejoicing! I love you all so dearly, my little children. With your many prayers and offerings you have decorated so many souls with the seed of conversion. So many hearts have bloomed just like fresh flowers. I thank you all, dear children. Keep living my messages with your eyes fixed on Heaven.

Message from Our Lady, October 3, 1991

Dear children, today, again, I call you all to decide for God. Satan is very busy and active trying to destroy souls. You, dear children, can make a difference in the world with your prayers, fasting and offerings. Do not get discouraged, but grow in goodness and purity. Continue praying, for these are hard times, and there is so much suffering, so much suffering. Pray, dear children, pray.

Message from Our Lady, October 8, 1991

Dear children, repent and be converted! Accept your little crosses that God sends your way. I am the Lady of Grace. Many graces are bestowed upon the faithful through my intercession. Therefore, trust in my intercession and love my Immaculate Heart. I love you so dearly, I love you so dearly. Trust in my intercession.

I am Your Mother Come from Heaven to Love You

Message from Our Lady, October 14, 1991

Janie saw Our Lady standing over a globe, and rays were streaming down from her hands illuminating all areas of the world. She was wearing a white dress, blue mantle, and there were twelve stars around her crown. Her crown was gold, and all around her was a golden haze.

Emmanating from her hands were different colors, but mostly white. The globe was also radiant and gold. Her mantle and dress were blowing in a breeze and waving over the whole world. Our Lady was smiling. Her light shown over the whole world.

Janie
What are you showing me, Blessed Mother? Why are you covering every area of the world?

Our Lady
I am the Mother of All Creation. I invite all my children to love one another, to live and work in harmony with one another. I am the Mother of All Creation, and I love you all, for you are my children.

Message from Jesus, October 22, 1991

Jesus
I am here for you always. I have given you My Precious Body and Blood so you would be redeemed. Take My Body and be nourished. Take My Blood and do not thirst. I am your strength. I am your hope. I am your teacher. Do not look anywhere else but to Me and My Father, for here lies eternal life. This is to be your strength always.

Janie
But what about those who do not feed on the Holy Eucharist?

Jesus
Men separated because of disobedience from the very beginning. My Father made one Church, and one people. Do not worry, I am with all my brothers and sisters. In the end there will be one Church, one people.

60

I am Your Mother Come from Heaven to Love You

Message from Our Lady, October 22, 1991

Dear children, pray to God all the time. Open your hearts to His graces, the graces with which He wishes to bless you. Children, you will never understand how important prayer is. Know, dear children, that God answers all prayers. Pray, pray, pray!

Message from Our Lady, October 31, 1991

OUR LADY SPEAKS TO US AS MOTHER OF COMPASSION AND LOVE

Our Lady was dressed in a beautiful robe of deep purple silk. She wore a deep purple cape with traces of gold on her cape and sleeves. Her dress was darker than her veil, and she wore a crown on her head.

Dear children, I, your heavenly Mother, come to you as a Mother of Compassion and a Mother of Love. I come to you, dear children, with an urgent message: Pray, children, pray!

Do not neglect my messages, for if you do I cannot help you. I will pray for you. I will pray for you. The Rosary is your weapon; pray it with faith, my children. I love you, I love you.

I am Your Mother Come from Heaven to Love You

Message from Our Mother of Compassion and Love
November 4, 1991

Dear children, peace and love, my dear children. Believe in my Son, for He is your strength. Listen to Him, and you will do God's Will.

Dear children, I am with you. Be obedient and pray for all the world, especially the unconverted. Peace, be filled with it, and love everyone that God sends your way. Your task is a difficult one, for you are called to love and believe with your hearts. I am with each one of you in a special way all the time.

Message from Our Mother of Compassion and Love
November 14, 1991

Dear children, be converted, be converted and live my messages! I am here to help you and to guide you. Open your hearts and love one another. Thank you for listening to my message.

Message from Our Mother of Compassion and Love
November 19, 1991

Our Lady came with the Rosary and the Scapular. On the Rosary, the Cross was lit up and a real Jesus was on the Cross with drops of Blood coming from His Wounds. The angels collected the Blood dropping from Jesus and flew off. The Scapular was also in a brilliant light and Our Lady said, "My children, sin no more. These are your tools. Clothe yourselves with them." Her message followed shortly after this.

Dear children, I have come from Heaven as your heavenly Mother. I have come to help you to be pure and holy, to prepare for the coming tribulation. Love one another. Love one another and be holy. Live a prayerful and holy life. Peace, peace and only peace.

I am Your Mother Come from Heaven to Love You

Message from Our Mother of Compassion and Love
November 25, 1991

Dear children, do not become discouraged. Many of you are becoming discouraged. When you feel this way pray your hardest, for the Almighty will give you His grace to go on.

Dear children, take refuge in my Immaculate Heart. Ask the Holy Spirit to enlighten you in times of difficulties. I am here for you, dear children, trust in my intercession. Through prayer you will receive your answers. Trust me and love my Son, love my Son.

Message from Our Mother of Compassion and Love
December 5, 1991

Dear children, glory to God in the Highest. Praised be His Holy Name forever and ever. Amen.

Prepare your hearts, little children, for My Son, for He is your salvation. Open your hearts and keep pure during this holy time. Be like shepherds on that Holy Night. Keep watch and pray for peace. I love you, my dear children, and I am always interceding for you.

Be pure and holy and ask for the gift of love, for this, little children, is the greatest gift. I am sad, because there is not enough love in this world; but you, my children, can make a difference. Be at prayer at all times and allow my Son's peace to live in your hearts. Thank you for listening to my message.

I am Your Mother Come from Heaven to Love You

Message from Our Lady of Guadeloupe
Feast of Our Lady of Guadeloupe, December 12, 1991

Dear children, peace and love! I am here at your side. I have come to help you and to teach you. Rejoice and love! Love, children, love, for this is the time when love will conquer all evil. Give one another the most precious gift one can offer my Son - which is love; that is all He asks for. Strive for love, and you will learn to love. You will learn to love! Thank you for listening to my message.

Message from Our Mother of Compassion and Love
December 16, 1991

Dear children, rejoice and be at peace. This is the time of rejoicing! Live Heaven on earth, doing God's Most Holy Will. May you spread the joy of my beloved Son to all the world around you.

Dear children, open your hearts and allow the love of my Son to fill you during this holy season. Rejoice! Rejoice, for God is with you. Thank you for listening to my message.

Message from Our Mother of Compassion and Love
January 6, 1992

Dear children, today, I come as the Queen of Peace and Queen of All Hearts. I love you all, my dear children, and I hold you all so tenderly in my Most Immaculate Heart. Pray, and be pure and holy. Love, children, love everyone. Pray for the unconverted and reach out to them with love. Pray together with your family. Thank you for listening to my message.

I am Your Mother Come from Heaven to Love You

Message from Our Mother of Compassion and Love
January 14, 1992

Dear children, take refuge in my Immaculate Heart, for I am here to help you and to sustain you from all the traps that the evil one is putting in your path.

Love, little children, love. Ask for a pure heart in your prayers, and the Almighty will grant you this prayer. I love you, dear children. I love you all, and I am here for you. Do not turn away from Heaven, but turn toward Heaven, for in Heaven you will find your paradise. Thank you for listening to my message.

Message from Our Mother of Compassion and Love
January 22, 1992

Dear children, come to your heavenly Mother and allow yourselves to be loved and cared for by me. Am I not your heavenly Mother? Am I not here to help you and lead you to Heaven? Do not allow yourselves to be frightened by the many problems that the evil one puts in your path. I ask you to look toward Heaven and to put your trust in God, the Almighty and Merciful Father.

I ask you, dear children, to allow yourselves to be loved by me, and I ask you to love yourselves as God loves you. In this way, when you love yourselves, you accept yourselves as God accepts you. Do not worry, little children, but trust, trust, trust! Thank you for listening to my message.

I am Your Mother Come from Heaven to Love You

Message from Our Mother of Compassion and Love
January 27, 1992

Dear children, today, I, your heavenly Mother, call you to pray for a loving heart. I am sad, because there is not enough love in the world. Please, dear children, help me to bring love into this unconverted world. Be obedient and spend more time in prayer.

Spend time with my Son in the Most Blessed Sacrament. He will help you and refresh you.

Spend more time praying and less time worrying and doubting. This world is in need of much conversion. Through your prayers and sacrifices this world will be converted. Thank you for listening to my message.

Message from Our Mother of Compassion and Love
February 6, 1992

Dear children, rejoice and be loving to all those souls that God puts in your path. Today, I ask you again, like never before, to live my messages and share them with others.

Dear children, today, I come to invite you to purity and to love. Do not worry, but take refuge in my Most Immaculate Heart and remain under my protection. Rejoice, rejoice, rejoice, for I am with you each step of the way! Thank you for listening to my message.

I am Your Mother Come from Heaven to Love You

Message from Our Mother of Compassion and Love
February 11, 1992

Dear children, today, I, your heavenly Mother, crown you, my children, with the crown of holiness. Remember, you were created in the likeness of your Creator, the Father Almighty. It is, then, your duty as a child of God to walk in holiness.

My Son died for you, so that you would be redeemed to God the Almighty. Through my Son you are given new life. Love my Son, then, and listen to Him. Trust in Him Who gave up His life for you, for He will lead you to eternal life. Thank you for listening to my message.

Message from Our Mother of Compassion and Love
February 17, 1992

Dear children, rejoice and do not become discouraged! Continue to pray and remember that God listens to your prayers.

Dear children, there are some of you who are worried about your loved ones. I am here to tell you do not worry, but pray and trust. Present all your prayers to God with faith. I love you, dear children, and I am here for you and to help you. Trust in my intercession and do not worry, but trust in your prayers. Remember, there is no room for fear and worry. Your loved ones will come to know my Son. Continue to pray for them. Thank you for listening to my message.

I am Your Mother Come from Heaven to Love You

Message from Our Mother of Compassion and Love
February 27, 1992

Dear children, peace and joy! Peace and joy! Be happy, little children, for I am here to take you to Heaven with me. When you pray, little children, you become like little beautiful flowers that illuminate all of Heaven.

Prayer is very important. Do not forget this, my little ones. Go then, and spread your love and prayers to all without hesitation. Thank you for listening to my message.

Message from Our Mother of Compassion and Love
March 3, 1992

Dear children, today, I invite you to open your hearts to my Son and trust Him. Embrace your Savior Who gave us His love. Look upon one another with His love, and spread this love where there is no love. Look at Him Who gave up His life for your salvation.

Model yourselves after my Son, and seek purity and holiness of heart. Detach yourselves and renounce everything, and accept your cross with joy. In doing this you will embrace the love of my Son and become holy and pure. Thank you for listening to my message.

Message from Our Mother of Compassion and Love
March 10, 1992

Dear children, I am the Queen of Peace, and I have come to bring peace to all my children throughout the world. I invite you to live this peace and share it with others. Be loving, and you will experience joy in your hearts.

Dear children, I invite you to pray more. Pray particularly in these hard times when there is so much violence and darkness around you, for these are troubled times.

I am Your Mother Come from Heaven to Love You

Message from March 10, 1992 (Continued)

Pray and fast, trust God with all your heart. I am here to help you and to lead you to holiness. Pray with love in your hearts, and love one another. Thank you for listening to my message.

Message from Our Mother of Compassion and Love
March 11, 1992

My Dear children, greetings to each one! I thank you for all your hard work and the suffering that you have endured. Know, my little ones, that God blesses all your efforts.

My little ones, today, I continue to invite you to prayer of the heart, where you surrender all to God, Who loves you so tenderly. Rejoice, my children, and continue to live my messages by your example. Be a living testimony to others; in this way, you will help me to bring others to conversion.

Prepare yourselves every day with strong prayer, and be loving to all whom God puts in your path. Be obedient, my little ones, and listen to my motherly teachings, for I am here to teach you about the love of God. If you respond to my requests and put my messages into practice, you won't have to worry about anything, for you will be under my shadow and protection. I will take care of you and your family. I will teach you everything about love and prayer. I will lead you closer to my Son's Heart.

My little children, you must open your hearts and decide for conversion. Learn to love God with all your hearts. Then, the Holy Spirit will enlighten you in all aspects of your lives. Pray, my children, pray. I love you all. Thank you for listening to my message.

I am Your Mother Come from Heaven to Love You

Message from Our Mother of Compassion and Love
March 24, 1992

Dear children, today, I invite you to pray for peace in the world. Extend your prayers to the entire world. Pray for peace for yourselves and your families. Trust in your prayers as you pray for peace.

Dear children, do not despair in your difficulties, for these are the times when much more suffering will take place, especially with those you love the most.

Pray, children, pray. Read Holy Scripture and live Holy Scripture, so that you may be protected from the hands of the evil one. My little ones, I am here to help you and to teach you. You must listen and live my messages. Pray and make God the most important friend you've ever had, for He is your true friend.

My children, I am the Queen of Peace and my Son is the Prince of Peace. Live this peace and share this peace with the world. Peace, peace, peace! Offer up all your prayers for peace. Thank you for listening to my message.

Message from Our Mother of Compassion and Love
March 30, 1992

Dear children, rejoice and pray for a joyful and loving heart. Purify your hearts through your love for my Son.

During this special time, spend more time with my Son and with your family, praying together for your needs. I am here to teach you how to love and pray. Trust in my presence with you. Thank you for listening to my message.

I am Your Mother Come from Heaven to Love You

Message from Our Mother of Compassion and Love
April 4, 1992

Dear children, peace, children, peace! Live your lives only for my Son. Abandon yourselves, abandon yourselves to God the Almighty. Live simply, and be at peace with one another.

Dear children, I love you all. You are most precious to my Immaculate Heart. I look forward to being with you and praying with you. Thank you for listening to my message.

Message from Our Mother of Compassion and Love
April 14,1992

Dear children, today, I invite you to live the Passion of my Son. Pray and fast. Pray for a pure heart and love one another.

Dear children, pray to God to help you in your struggles, for some of you struggle needlessly. You struggle because you don't take time to pray. When you pray, you don't believe in your prayer. (She meant you pray without faith).

Pray and fast, dear children, for prayer opens up your heart. Pray together as a family. Pray the Rosary every day. Thank you for listening to my message.

I am Your Mother Come from Heaven to Love You

Message from Our Mother of Compassion and Love
April 20, 1992

Dear children, peace, and rejoice in my risen Son, for He has risen to give you new life!

Today, I invite you to peace and to share this peace with the rest of the world. Put all your struggles aside and pray for peace, for the world is ready for peace. Believe in this peace that I invite you to live, and share it. Put all worries and doubts aside, for these things put distance between you and God. I am the Queen of Peace, and this peace that I invite you to live comes from God. Thank you for listening to my message.

Message from Our Mother of Compassion and Love
April 30, 1992

Dear children, rejoice, rejoice, rejoice for I am here to help you and lead you to Heaven! All you have to do is open your hearts, and listen to the voice of the Holy Spirit within you.

My little ones, trust in my intercession and take refuge in my Immaculate Heart. Be at peace and pray your Rosaries, for the Rosary is your weapon. Again, I say, trust in my intercession. I love you, my children, I love you all. Thank you for listening to my message.

I am Your Mother Come from Heaven to Love You

Message from Our Mother of Compassion and Love
May 5, 1992

Dear children, today, I, your heavenly Mother, invite you to a new life of prayer and purity. Open your hearts, dear children, and abandon yourselves to God. Decide for conversion and accept all your crosses with joy.

My little ones, listen to your heavenly Mother, and allow your lives to be transformed into lives of prayer. Accept and follow the path that leads to eternal life. Do not be afraid to convert, but convert and God will remove all your fears. Thank you for listening to my message.

Message from Our Mother of Compassion and Love
Mother's Day, May 10, 1992

To All Mothers,

I greet and bring the blessing from God to each of you! Special blessings are given to each one of you. I ask you to continue doing the work of my Son. Love the gifts that you have been blessed with, which are your children. Love them and nurture their souls, and prepare them for the Kingdom of God. Know that a beautiful, heavenly crown is being prepared for you in Heaven. Each time you bring your children to God, a divine jewel is added to your crown.

Do not be afraid to be a good mother and lead your children in the right direction. I know that your job in bringing your children to God is a difficult task. It is important that you remember that God has given you all the graces necessary to be that heavenly mother that God intended for you to be.

Know that I am praying for each of you all the time and helping you to bring yourselves and your family to God the Father. I ask and invite you to pray for one another; and please pray for all those poor mothers who do not know my Son and for those mothers who reject Him.

73

I am Your Mother Come from Heaven to Love You

Message from Our Mother of Compassion and Love
May 21, 1992

Dear children, open your hearts and allow God to help you. Pray, my children, pray, for prayer opens your hearts, and prayer brings you peace. God wants to give you His peace. Little children, there is no happiness or joy without God's peace.

You pray and ask God's help, but you do not have open hearts. You ask for God's forgiveness, but you refuse to forgive others. How can God help you, my children, if you do not trust Him?

Abandon yourselves, abandon yourselves and God will help you. Listen to me, listen to me, for time is running out! Come to God now, little children, not tomorrow, but now! Thank you for listening to my message.

Message from Our Mother of Compassion and Love
May 26, 1992

Dear children, peace, little children, peace! I come to pray for you, for some of you are fearful of the signs and wonders that surround you. Know that you are in the midst of the great tribulation. Much suffering will take place with many of your loved ones.

Do not worry, for I am here with you. Nothing will harm you if you live Holy Scripture. Rejoice, little children, and continue to pray, for prayer is your strength.

I am here, I am here, do not be afraid. You, my children, are the light of the world. Allow that light to shine, shine, shine! I love you, my little precious ones. Thank you for listening to my message.

I am Your Mother Come from Heaven to Love You

Message from Our Mother of Compassion and Love
June 1, 1992

Dear children, I am here to help you to prepare for the coming of my beloved Spouse, the Holy Spirit. I ask each one of you to offer all your prayers, masses, novenas, as a means of preparation. You will be blessed if you respond to my request. I love you all, my children, and I want your hearts to be open to receive all the blessings from Heaven. Rejoice and praise God, praise God! Thank you for listening to my message.

Message from Our Mother of Compassion and Love
June 11,1992

Dear children, today, I, your heavenly Mother, invite you to open your hearts and prepare your hearts for my Son, Jesus. He is calling each one of you. He is gathering all people from all nations through my intercession to come and join His army that He has been preparing throughout time.

Dear children, time is short. I have mentioned this on several occasions; believe and prepare. I call you again to prayer and fasting, to conversion, to total abandonment. These are your spiritual tools that will protect you from Satan. Thank you for listening to my message.

I am Your Mother Come from Heaven to Love You

Message from Our Mother of Compassion and Love
June 16, 1992

Dear children, today, I invite you to prayer of the heart. Spend time in prayer and less time talking about prayer. Be silent, and you will hear the voice of God in your hearts.

Pray and fast, and be humble of heart. Love one another. Pray to God for a loving heart, in this way you will love all people that God puts in your path.

My children, the harvest of salvation is here. Believe, repent, and be converted, and you will have eternal salvation! Thank you for listening to my message.

Message from Our Mother of Compassion and Love
June 22, 1992

Dear children, today, I invite you again to continue to pray and fast. I need all your sacrifices to help convert many souls. There are so many of my children who are not yet converted.

My precious ones, I would not ask you for so much prayer and fasting if it wasn't of great importance. Know that as you pray and fast, your own hearts become more open to the Will of God. Prayer opens the heart and fasting brings about your own purification.

Help me, my dear children, help me, and together you and I will help to bring much conversion throughout the world. Thank you for listening to my message.

I am Your Mother Come from Heaven to Love You

Message from Our Mother of Compassion and Love
June 30, 1992

Dear children, greetings to all! Today, I want to thank you for your prayers and sacrifices. There has been much conversion throughout the world.

Do not worry about anything, but pray for peace in the world. Offer up novenas as a means of penance, for there is much spiritual healing in these devotions. Offer novenas frequently in your prayers. Peace, peace, peace. I love you, dear ones. Thank you for listening to my message.

Message from Our Mother of Compassion and Love
July 6, 1992

Dear children, today, I, your heavenly Mother, invite you to return back to God. Many of you, my little children, have listened and accepted salvation in your lives. To you, I say, thank you!

Continue to pray for those who refuse to accept God's love and mercy. Time is short, and the suffering continues due to lack of faith and love.

To you who are struggling with your faith, have courage. Be converted, be converted! Thank you for listening to my message.

Message from Our Mother of Compassion and Love
July 13, 1992

Dear children, I am here to ask and invite you to continue praying for conversion, peace and love in the world.

Dear children, many of you have not taken my messages of the family to heart. You continue to allow your children freedom which endangers their souls. You continue to watch endless hours of television.

77

I am Your Mother Come from Heaven to Love You

Message from July 13, 1992 (Continued)

Many of you have not been praying as a family. This saddens my Immaculate Heart, for I am in need of your family prayers. Please, open your hearts and decide for prayer, for if you do not pray, you endanger your souls.

Today, I ask you to pray and to live as a holy family. Ask St. Joseph to intercede for you and your family. He will help you, and he will pray for you. Pray, children, pray. Thank you for listening to my message.

Message from Our Mother of Compassion and Love
July 23, 1992

Dear children, pray and trust. Be at peace, for having peace in your hearts is so important. Many of you are unhappy; to you, I say, pray and trust. God knows all your needs. Be open to His love and blessings. Be at peace, and share this peace with others. Thank you for listening to my message.

Message from Our Mother of Compassion and Love
August 10, 1992

Dear children, today, I invite you to take refuge in my Immaculate Heart. Pray for a pure heart and a willing spirit. In this way you will do God's Holy Will. Make God's Will your own through your trust in Him.

Remain under my mantle, and together through your prayers and sacrifices, you will help me to usher in the reign of my Son and the triumph of my Immaculate Heart.

Thank you, my little children, I love you all. Thank you for listening to my message.

I am Your Mother Come from Heaven to Love You

Message from Our Mother of Compassion and Love
Feast of the Assumption, August 15, 1992

Dear children, rejoice, my chosen ones, and come to celebrate with me on my feast day. Come, my little ones, and bring all your prayers and sacrifices. Offer them up to God with all your love.

My little ones, today, I ask that you give thanks to the Almighty Father for allowing me to be with you for such a long time. Be grateful, my children, and show your gratitude by doing all that I am asking you. Be loving, be prayerful, be obedient. Pray for purity of the heart, for when you pray with a pure heart, God answers your prayers. He loves purity.

My little flowers, you wonder how to obtain a pure heart. My little ones, you do this through the sacrament of Reconciliation. That is why I ask you to receive this sacrament frequently. Rejoice, for today I will bless you all, my little ones, in a special way. I ask each one of you to bring me all your concerns, that I may present them to God. Rejoice, for you will feel the presence of my beloved Son Who rejoices with me. Be thankful on this special day for my glorious Assumption into Heaven. Love your Heavenly Queen and trust in my intercession. I am the glory of the New Jerusalem, Queen of Heaven and Earth.

Rejoice, and give thanks to God, that He has blessed you with my presence on earth. I am coming to many throughout the world. I am preparing a spiritual ark, my little ones, that has been formed from your many, many prayers and offerings. Today, I wish to thank you, my children. You have been so helpful with your prayers, and in helping me to bring many new souls to my beloved Son, Jesus. Know that each day, many souls are being converted through your prayers.

Beware! Satan is very angry, for he is growing weak. The weaker he gets, the more aggressive he becomes. His goal is to destroy your family, so pray together as a family. Love and forgive one another, for the family that prays together, grows together in faith, peace, unity and strength. Do not be afraid of Satan, for your prayers dissolve all his evil tricks that he puts in your path.

Message from August 15, 1992 (Continued)

That is why, my children, I ask you again and again to attend Holy Mass together as a family. (She means daily). Also, receive the sacrament of Reconciliation, pray your Rosary, spend time with my Son in Adoration, read and live Holy Scripture. If you do this, my children, you will have a place with me in paradise. Rejoice, rejoice, rejoice and give glory to God forever and ever. Thank you for listening to my message.

Message from Our Mother of Compassion and Love
August 17, 1992

Dear children, peace and joy! My greetings to all!

Today, my children, I invite you to continue to pray and fast. You, dear children, ask much of God. You must make sacrifices to receive answers to your prayers. You obtain your answers by means of prayer and fasting. God is ready to answer all your prayers according to His Holy Will.

Dear children, do not grow tired of my asking you to be converted. Conversion brings you closer to God. As you begin to convert, your hearts begin to bloom like beautiful heavenly flowers. Be obedient, my children, and respond to my call to prayer, fasting and conversion. Thank you, my little ones, thank you.

I am Your Mother Come from Heaven to Love You

Message from Our Mother of Compassion and Love
August 24, 1992

Dear children, greetings to all! Today, I invite you again in a special way to pray more and to trust God with your prayers. Spend more time with my Son; allow Him to help you to draw closer to His loving heart.

My little ones, do not be afraid to reach out to one another when you need prayers or love. You are all my children, and I want you to live together in harmony and in love; that is why I ask you to pray and to love one another.

My dear ones, I ask that you listen to my plea to pray more, to trust God with your prayer. If you do not have trust in God, you cannot pray with a trusting heart. Pray and trust, pray and trust. Thank you for listening to my message.

Message from Our Mother of Compassion and Love
September 3, 1992

Dear children, greetings, my precious ones! You are so special to me. I thank each one for coming together to pray.

Today, I wish to share with you that my Son wants to use each one of you to help me through your prayers to convert all people. My Son is calling all people to come together and form one body in Him.

Be united, not only with your family but with all people. Be a neighbor to all souls that you meet. By embracing all people, you embrace my Son. I love you, my children. God gave you all to me from the Cross to teach you and guide you to my Son. Trust in my intercession, and know that I am with each one of you. Continue to pray, trusting God with your prayers. Do not fear anything. Let there be no room for fear in your hearts, only trust. Be at peace then. Pray, pray, pray! Thank you for listening to my message.

I am Your Mother Come from Heaven to Love You

Message from Our Mother of Compassion and Love
Birthday of Our Lady, September 8, 1992

Dear children, greetings to all! Thank you for responding to my call. Today, my children, the Church celebrates my feast day. You, too, are called to celebrate with the Church.

I wish to share my joy with you. So many of my children are coming to God for the first time. I am so happy and joyful for your obedience, for it is through your many prayers and sacrifices that many of my children are coming to know my Son. Thank you, my children, for all your prayers. I hold you all close to my bosom. Rejoice and live the Good News. Thank you. Thank you.

Message from Our Lord Jesus in the Blessed Sacrament and Our Mother of Compassion and Love, September 14, 1992

Janie called Doctor T. Doctor T., always calm because she knew Our Lady was directing the project, nevertheless faced some seemingly overwhelming problems concerning the Peace Flight to Russia, and she said to Janie, "Our Lord and His Mother know what is in my heart. Please ask Them if They have a word for me."

While Janie was in adoration before the Blessed Sacrament, she heard these words for Doctor T. : "Peace, joy and blessings from Heaven. Jesus and Mary are with you each step of the way. God is pleased."

Janie was invited to make a pilgrimage to Russia. This message and several in October (the actual month of the pilgrimage) refer to this event.

I am Your Mother Come from Heaven to Love You

Message from Our Mother of Compassion and Love
Triumph of the Cross Feast, September 14, 1992

Dear children, greetings to all! I love you all for your commitment to being here today. My dear little ones, come to me, come to me, that I may console your wounded and confused hearts. Do not worry about anything, do not be afraid. I am here, I am here.

Pray to God for His strength in your difficulties. He will give you the grace to endure every trial that you are suffering. My little ones, pray for the conversion of all sinners and for those souls that do not yet know my Son. Endure you sufferings a little longer and offer them for the conversion of the world. I love you all. Thank you for listening to my message.

Message from Our Mother of Compassion and Love
September 24, 1992

Dear children, greetings, my little ones! I am so happy to see you. Today, I call you to peace and love. Do not concern yourselves with anything. Be at peace, open your hearts, allow God's love to enter your hearts.

God wants to share His Kingdom with you. You must remember that you do not have to search for God's Kingdom anywhere else other than your hearts, for God's Kingdom is within you. Peace and love. Thank you for listening to my message.

Message from Our Mother of Compassion and Love
September 29, 1992

Dear children, greetings to each one of you! Welcome to my Sorrowful and Immaculate Heart. I love you all, my dearest children. Today, I ask you to pray, pray, pray!

I am Your Mother Come from Heaven to Love You

Message from Our Mother of Compassion and Love
October 6, 1992

Dear children, greetings to all my beloved children! Thank you all for your commitment to coming today. Know that God blesses all your efforts, for He knows your needs.

I invite you to receive all the gifts that God is blessing you with. Open your hearts especially to my message today. Pray your Rosaries with devotion. My time is short on earth, and I am preparing you for the tribulation. During this time, you are being purified through your suffering. Do not resist your purification, but accept it with an open and joyful heart. Love one another, and love your neighbor always. Peace, peace, peace. Thank you for listening to my message.

Message from Our Lord Jesus in the Blessed Sacrament
Lourdes, France, October 11, 1992

This is a very important event in your lives. Know that you will never understand the special event that is about to unfold.

You, My dear ones, are making history that will sound around the world from nation to nation. You are proclaiming God's Kingdom on earth by joining together My Most Sacred Heart and the Most Immaculate Heart of My Mother. Through this gathering you are living witnesses that I am King of all Nations, together with the reign of My Most Holy Mother.

This event will join together your separated and long lost sister, Russia. You will be embracing one another for the first time in history. You, My children, have dissolved the Iron Curtain with your many prayers and sacrifices. Go, then, and march toward your sister and love her and share your faith with her.

Go, My children. You represent all of Heaven by your heroic efforts. You are those soldiers that have been picked and blessed by the Queen of Peace herself.

I am Your Mother Come from Heaven to Love You

Message from Our Lord Jesus, October 11, 1992 (Continued)

Go and sing loudly as you approach your sister, Russia, singing, "Onward Christian Soldiers." Go marching with the Cross of Jesus, King of all Nations, and the Queen of Heaven guiding this faith journey. Go and make peace. The Heavens rejoice! The Heavens rejoice!

Message from Our Mother of Compassion and Love
Lisbon, Portugal, October 12, 1992

Dear children, greetings to each one of you! You, my children, have brought joy to my heart through your many prayers and sacrifices. You are all so precious to me, and you need not worry about anything.

You have been chosen for this journey of faith. Yes, my children, this is a faith journey, and you must pray, for Satan is very angry, and he will try to destroy you by putting many obstacles in your path. He cannot touch you, for you have a multitude of angels protecting you. St. Michael is guiding this faith journey.

Be at peace and do not worry about anything, but pray, pray, pray. I love you, my children. Remember, my little ones, the Rosary is your weapon. Thank you for listening to my message.

I am Your Mother Come from Heaven to Love You

Message from Our Mother of Compassion and Love
Portugal, October 14, 1992

My dear children, you have the blessings of my Son, and I myself bless you to go out and have a joyful day. My dear little ones, pray more to the Holy Spirit, for God has sent you the Holy Spirit to give you His wisdom.

Pray more and continue to put your complete trust in God, the Father Almighty, for He is the One Who directs all your actions.

My little ones, you will never understand the importance of prayer. Pray, my children, pray, for prayer is what will remove all the obstacles that the evil one is trying to put in your path. Prayer, my children, opens up your heart to be in complete oneness with God. So, I say to you, pray, pray, pray! Thank you for listening to my message.

Message from Our Lady of Guadeloupe
Prague, October 16, 1992

My dear children, greetings and love to each one of you! My children, you are reaching your destination. Prepare much with strong prayer, for the evil one continues to make your faith journey a difficult one.

I am here to remind you once more: do not worry about anything. Do not fear anything, for worry and fear will only serve to distract you from your mission.

Rejoice, my little ones. Am I not here? Are you not all under my motherly mantle? Rejoice, rejoice, rejoice!

Do not have the smallest worry. You should only be concerned with being in a loving and prayerful spirit.

Your sister Russia, my children, needs your love and faith. My children, I, too, am embracing my children in Russia. Let us go together and embrace her with God's love. Thank you for listening to my message.

I am Your Mother Come from Heaven to Love You

Message from Our Lady of Fatima
Red Square, Moscow, October 18, 1992

Precisely at the moment that a small image of Our Lady of Fatima was being crowned by John Haffert, Janie saw Our Lady of Fatima appear over the square wearing a crown. Light streamed from her heart flooding the square and then bounced up and outwards in all directions.

These were Our Lady's words: "Thank you for your obedience and prayers. You, my children, have overcome many obstacles by obedience and prayer. You have brought so much joy to my heart. Know that your rewards are great in Heaven, for you have pleased God. Remain small in the eyes of the world, that you may be great in the eyes of God."

Message from Our Mother of Compassion and Love
St. Petersburg, October 19, 1992

My dear children, greetings to each one of you! I want to thank you for all your hard work and all the sufferings that you have endured. You have God's blessing for all your efforts.

My little ones, it is important that you remember how much I continue to need your prayers and perseverance. Many of you are getting discouraged and tired. Your frustration tolerance is low, and you have been unkind to others around you. I know you have met and put up with many difficulties, but you know the Way of the Cross is not easy.

You must remember that you are children of the light and that light must shine for others to see. I have been with you each step of the way, just like I was with the disciples when my Son ascended into Heaven. Trust me, my children, for I will not leave you, not even for one moment.

I am Your Mother Come from Heaven to Love You

Message from St. Petersburg, October 19, 1992 (Continued)

Many of you have relaxed and believe that you have accomplished your mission. My dear children, your mission has just begun to unfold. Remember, you are prayer warriors, and you must not grow tired of prayer. I tell you this, for many of you are not in a prayerful spirit or attitude.

Beware, my little ones. Satan is trying so hard to take your peace away. He has succeeded with many of you who are questioning why you came and what you should do next. You are getting distracted with all these questions. You are here, because you have responded *yes* to my call, and what happens next is not for you to worry about.

My children, you have been hand picked by God for this peace journey. You came to bring God's love to Russia. She has not yet been converted. She continues to need much prayer and many sacrifices. You have seen her woundedness and how starved she is for God's love. Russia lives in darkness, and many of my children in Russia saw and felt your love, and I thank you deeply.

I want to thank you again and again and ask you to please do not become discouraged. I am with you, and all of Heaven rejoices as you continue in this peace journey, spreading your love to those souls that God has put in your path. Do not give up but pray and trust. Never forget that prayer is your strength, for prayer opens your heart to the Will of God. I love you all so dearly. Rejoice and continue serving God with a joyful heart. Thank you for listening to my message.

I am Your Mother Come from Heaven to Love You

Message from Jesus in the Blessed Sacrament
St. Alphonsus Church, Rome, October 24, 1992, 11:20 a.m.

My dear ones, peace to all! I bless each step you take. Be at peace with one another. I have sent you many small and big crosses in your journey. Some of you have accepted the crosses, but many of My children have rejected these crosses and have continued to complain. Bear your crosses a little bit longer, and you will give thanks to God for all these crosses, for the way to the Father is the Way of the Cross.

Love My Mother is what I ask of each of you, and hold Her close to your heart. Love and adore My Sacred Heart, for when each one of you learns to love and adore both Hearts, you will begin to know the love and mercy of My Father. The love of the United Hearts is what will lead you to the heart of My Father.

My dear faithful ones, for a long time now My Mother has been preparing each one of you to take and live this peace journey. Open your hearts and do not allow your love to grow weak and tired. If you only knew the glory that you are giving My Father and the honor that My Mother receives as you continue your peace journey, if you understood the importance of your mission, you would give thanks to the Almighty Father for all the crosses and sufferings that you have endured.

Pray, My faithful ones, pray, for prayer will help you to keep the love and unity that is the focus of this journey. Do not be distracted with anything that comes your way, but pray and trust. Again, I say, pray and trust, and you will have victory over Satan. Remain pure, loving and humble, for these are the signs of God's people.

I am Your Mother Come from Heaven to Love You

Message from Jesus , October 25, 1992, 6:35 p.m., Rome
Vision of the Two Hearts

My dear ones, you have made Our Hearts radiant through your obedience, sacrifices and love, and I say to you: thank you, thank you, thank you!

Jesus and Mary were very happy with this pilgrimage, and with all the prayers, sacrifices and sufferings that we endured, as well as those that were offered by others for the success of this pilgrimage.

Message from Our Mother of Compassion and Love
November 5, 1992

Dear children, greetings to all! Today, I, your heavenly Mother, invite you to continue to persevere in your prayers. Do not have any concerns, God knows all your needs. Trust Him.

My children, seek God's Most Holy Will in everything, for His Will is different from your own will. Be content with your faith journey and remain close as a family.

Pray with me everyday before the Blessed Sacrament. Spend some time in prayer telling my Son all your needs. He will bless you, He will bless you!

I love you, my children, and I am with each one of you. Remain in the spirit of prayer. God will bless you in all your efforts. Peace, peace, my little ones. Thank you for listening to my message.

I am Your Mother Come from Heaven to Love You

Message from Our Mother of Compassion and Love
November 11, 1992

Dear children, greetings to all! I love you all so dearly. Today, I invite you to prayer of the heart. Abandon yourselves completely to God. Have faith in all your prayers and do not doubt.

Pray to the Holy Spirit for enlightenment to do the Holy Will of God. The Holy Spirit will help you and guide you. Pray, my children, pray! Thank you for listening to my message.

Message from Jesus in the Blessed Sacrament
November 26, 1992, 2:40 a.m.
Thanksgiving Morning

Beloved child,

Do not be surprised at the fiery ordeal which comes upon you to purify you, but rejoice insofar as you share in My suffering. Trust Me, your beloved Savior, and endure all your suffering for My love for you.

Message from Our Mother of Compassion and Love
December 1, 1992

Dear children, today, I invite you to empty your hearts and allow God to fill you with His love. You come to pray, because you need guidance, and you long for peace in your heart.

My little ones, I am here with you in a very special way. I have come to instruct and to teach you how to pray from the heart. Prayer of the heart means being open to God's Will and trusting Him in all your prayers. Do not become discouraged when your prayer is not answered right away. Pray for faith, and to be able to recognize the mercy of God, for He loves you so much, and He listens to all your prayers.

Message from December 1, 1992 (Continued)

I ask you to prepare in a special way when you return to your home, and to spend quiet time in prayer with God. Pray for a prayerful spirit, and be focused on nothing else except prayer.

Be at peace with one another, and live in God's love. Choose the road that leads to holiness, and be converted! When you decide for holiness, you will become holy. Choose Heaven, and live as God's children, doing His holy deeds on earth.

Listen to your heavenly Mother, and be attentive to all that I tell you, for the day will come when I no longer will be with you. Little children, I want to teach you about God's love. I want to teach you about holiness and purity of heart. I want to lead you closer to my Son, Jesus.

I love you, all my children. Pray as a family, always, and never doubt in my love for you. My love and my intercession is always with you. Thank you for listening to my message.

I am Your Mother Come from Heaven to Love You

Message from Jesus, December 4, 1992, 5:45 a.m.
Home; in the prayer room

Janie
Praised be Jesus forever and ever. Amen.

Jesus, please give me a sign that you are here.

Jesus
My child, I am here with you. Have no doubt, but prepare to write.

Then He asked, "Are you ready to write?"

Janie
Yes, my Jesus.

Jesus
Here is a teaching on the family, husband and wife. The family was created and blessed by God, therefore, the family is a holy union. God created man and woman, so that together they would be fruitful and multiply through their love for one another.

In the beginning, God created all creatures to be fruitful and multiply, so it was for this reason that He created man and woman. God instructed man and woman to live in His love and to be obedient to His guidance. He provided them with everything they needed. Both man and woman lived in peace and in true happiness, loving one another. God loved them so much, that He gave them freedom, which was the free will to choose between good and evil. This was God's gift to humanity: to love all His children with unconditional love.

You, My little one, teach your family about God's unconditional love. I will teach you everything you need to know, so that you may harvest the hearts of the family. This is all for now.

Janie
Thank you, my Lord. I love you, Jesus, I love you.

Jesus
And We love you. (Our Lady was with Him).

93

I am Your Mother Come from Heaven to Love You

Message from Our Mother of Compassion and Love, December 8, 1992, 9:45 a.m.
Feast of The Immaculate Conception

Our Lady
My daughter, you are unhappy.

Janie
Yes, my Lady, for I am depending more on myself and not enough on your guidance.

Our Lady
My daughter, I am here with you. My little one, you are suffering much for the conversion of your family and your own conversion. Do not be sad on this beautiful day. Rejoice, and prepare to write.

Janie
Oh come, Most Holy Immaculate Mary, Mother Most Holy, and fill your children with divine words from Heaven!

Our Lady
My dear children, greetings to each one of you in this holy season. God is calling you to prepare for the coming of my Son. Praise be to God, for all of Heaven adores Him. He Who is mighty has done great things for all of creation. Holy is His Name.

My children, as you gather together on this my feast day, I, your Mother, come to teach you about prayer and how to obtain purity of heart. I am the gate that leads you to my Son, He is the Way that leads you to Heaven.

God has made me the Mother of All Humanity, Mother of Compassion and Love. In doing this, God has blessed you with His presence among you through the Two United Hearts.

As the Immaculate Conception, I come to teach love and purity, for God is calling all humanity to be reconciled back to Him through my Son, Jesus. I am the gate that leads you to my Son through my Immaculate Heart.

Stop turning away from God and open your hearts to His calling, for God yearns for your goodness and purity. Come, my children, let me lead you to my Son, Who will lead you to Heaven. Come, do not hesitate, God is calling you.

My dear ones, awake from the sleep of darkness and awake to the hour of great light of the love of God. Stop sinning, stop sinning and ask for my intercession for purity of heart!

To my beloved priests, assist your heavenly Mother in bringing all my children back to the love of God. For the hour will come when it will be too late! To you, my priests, I call you also, come, walk through the gate that leads all humanity to my Son through my Immaculate Heart. In the end the Two United Hearts will triumph!

My children, I am your Mother of Compassion and Love, trust in my intercession. I am here to help you to obtain purity of heart and holiness through means of prayer. I hold you all dear to my Immaculate Heart. Thank you for listening to my message.

I am Your Mother Come from Heaven to Love You

Message from Our Lady of Guadeloupe
December 12, 1992, 7:45 a.m.
Feast of Our Lady of Guadeloupe

My Little Daughter,

Why are you sad? I desire that you rejoice with me on this beautiful day. I know, my little daughter, my smallest one, that you continue to suffer, but I am here to tell you that you have found favor with God. Your husband and children are also favored by God; that is why you suffer, so that your hearts will be truly open to God, Who has called you to a mission to live the Gospel and to share it with others.

My littlest daughter, I need your help to go out and be an example (a good wife) to other families and to share with them what I am teaching you. God has graced you with a divine responsibility, and you have a mission, therefore, do not allow yourself to doubt and grow weak. God has chosen many souls for a special calling to be examples of the Gospel and to be messengers. There are many of my children that I have come to. These are the messengers that are being visited by my Son and by me. You are one of those messengers. Trust in God, and worry about nothing, for He will never give you more than what you can handle.

My little daughter, I want you to share with others all that you are being taught by the Two United Hearts, Who are one with God. I am the Mother of All Creation. I love all my children. I came as Queen of Peace and to teach all my children to pray for peace in their hearts, for where there is peace, there is also joy. This world is in so much need of peace and conversion and to return back to my Son.

On this day, I visited my little son, Juan Diego, and to him I asked for a Church to be built in my honor. To him I came as *Nuestra Senora de Guadeloupe*. During this time there was so much need for conversion, so much blood shed. Many of my innocent children were being sacrificed. Today, the horror continues through the sacrifice of millions of innocent infants.

This horror must stop! If not, many souls will not go to Heaven. To my little son, Juan Diego, I gave the sign of my tilma, that to this day remains untouched by human destruction. To you, my little daughter, I have left you my image and statue that you always remember me. To my son, Juan Diego, I asked him to remain obedient and pure, and to you, I make the same request.

Message from December 12, 1992 (Continued)

I love you, my little daughter, and God is very pleased that you promised to forget all your woundedness and all who have wounded you. You have a desire to begin all over, remembering no past woundedness, and to live in total abandonment, loving yourself, and your family with God's love. This humble attitude has brought much rejoicing in Heaven.

Prepare then, my little daughter, and remain small and humble, for this is the holy season, when God sent His only begotten Son for the salvation of the world. On that glorious night the shepherds followed the bright star that led them to Bethlehem, to a poor and humble stable, where they found the Infant Son of the Most High God, laying in a manger. The shepherds were filled with joy and peace.

In this way, be like the shepherds that followed that bright star two thousand years ago. Allow that moment to come alive in your heart, for your bright star is my Son. He is the star that you must follow. Live in Him, remain in Him, be Christ like, and you will know the peace that the world cannot give. I am the Mother of All Creation, Queen of Peace.

Long live Jesus, my Son, Prince of Peace, forever and ever. To Him all glory forever and ever.

I am Your Mother Come from Heaven to Love You

Message from Our Mother of Compassion and Love
December 17, 1992

My dear children, peace and greetings to all! Thank you for your commitment to coming to be with me. You have God's blessings.

My children, today, I ask each one of you to pray for peace and unity in your families, in your neighborhood, your Church, and your country. Unity is so important, but you must have peace, then unity follows.

My children, my time with you is short. I have been teaching you and guiding you. The day will come when you will have to be with me in faith, when I will no longer be visiting you. Be strong and grow in faith and in love. I will always be with you in spirit and in prayer.

During this time I have been teaching you about the love and mercy of God. I have taught you about the importance of prayer and fasting and how you obtain answers to your prayers when you pray and fast. I taught you to be loving to one another, especially loving your family.

I love you, my little ones, and I invite you to continue to be enlightened by the Holy Spirit. Pray for the grace to do God's Will in all situations; then you will be able to embrace all your small and big crosses with the love of God. Pray every day to the Holy Spirit, Who will give you the divine wisdom and true discernment to be able to recognize things that are of God. Begin your day with the prayer to the Holy Spirit and end your day with the prayer to the Holy Spirit, for the essence of the Holy Spirit is the heart of God.

My children, do not become bored and lazy when you need to be praying. Prayer is so important, for prayer changes hearts and brings about hope. Therefore, pray, pray, pray, for God listens to all your prayers.

My children, continue to prepare your hearts for my Son during this holy season. Do not be concerned about the gifts you give to one another. The most important gift is the gift of love and true friendship in God. Do not waste your time in buying gifts that are expensive, but give from the heart the gift of love; it costs nothing, and it is priceless.

I am Your Mother Come from Heaven to Love You

Message from December 17, 1992 (Continued)

Remain pure and humble. Rejoice, rejoice and spend time as a family, loving one another with God's love! Thank you for listening to my message.

Message from Our Mother of Compassion and Love
December 22, 1992

Dear children, greetings to all and I thank you deeply for your commitment to gather in prayer with me! I love you all so dearly.

Today, I thank you for all your prayers and sacrifices. Many of you are turning more toward God and away from the world. This is pleasing to God.

My little ones, some of you are having a hard time praying. Do not become discouraged but continue to pray, and you will find peace.

My children, your hearts are like beautiful flower buds that are ready to blossom. When you pray, your hearts become fully blossomed with sweet fragrance that reaches the throne of God. So pray, pray, pray!

My children, decide for conversion and for purity of heart. Listen to my messages and let them penetrate your hearts. Do not talk about my messages, but live them. Spend quiet time meditating on my messages, and ask my Son, Jesus, to help you in understanding the importance of all my messages. Talk less and pray more, and in this way the Holy Spirit will enlighten your hearts to know the Will of God.

Prepare your hearts for the coming of my Son, Jesus. In a few more days the world will celebrate the birth of my Son. It saddens my heart that many will miss the true meaning of their Savior's birth. Many do not want to acknowledge His birth. Many hate my Son and utter horrible things about Him. This pierces my heart. So, I turn to you, my children, who love my Son, and ask for your prayers. Together, our prayers will help those hearts that are full of darkness. I invite you to prepare your own hearts through being reconciled to one another and to God. This is the most precious gift that you can give my Son.

99

I am Your Mother Come from Heaven to Love You

Message from December 22, 1992 (Continued)

My children, Christmas is a holy day and must be honored as a holy day. Be together with your family, pray together. Do not allow Satan to distract you from the peace of my Son. Do not quarrel on this day, but pray that on this holy day you will begin a new life with my Son. Let this be a new beginning for you and your family.

I wish to thank all the parents for bringing their children. My Son has blessed all your children. To the children I say: listen and obey your parents, and God will bless you in every aspect of your lives. I pray peace, love, and holiness for all. Thank you for listening to my message.

Message from Our Mother of Compassion and Love
January 7, 1993

Dear children, greetings! Thank you all for coming to spend time in prayer. Trust in all your prayers and have no doubt. God will bless you, God will bless you.

Today, I urgently invite you to continue to pray for peace in the world. Pray, little children, pray like never before, for Satan is very active in his efforts to separate you from God. Do not become discouraged with all your suffering and your crosses, but pray, pray, pray!

Remember, my little ones, prayer is your strength. Trust God in all your prayers. He is always with you. He never leaves you, but when you stop praying and trusting in Him, then it is you who leaves Him. Never stop praying, for prayer helps you to remain with God forever. Thank you for listening to my message.

I am Your Mother Come from Heaven to Love You

Message from Our Mother of Compassion and Love
January 12, 1993, 7:50 a.m.

My Dear children, greetings to all! Thank you for your commitment to be here today. I thank you, again, with deep gratitude.

My dear ones, today, I invite you to continue to pray for peace in the world. Pray with me, my children, so that together you and I may lead others to my Son.

Open your hearts, my little ones, and decide for conversion, for God wishes to bless each one of you. Do not allow your sufferings to distract you from doing the Will of God, for God knows all your needs. Trust Him and abandon yourselves completely to Him, that He may be able to help you. Be loving to one another and help one another. Be humble, be obedient in all that I am asking you to do. Live my messages and help your families and encourage them to trust in my intercession. I hold you all so dear to my Most Immaculate Heart.

My children, my time with you is short, so have faith in my messages. Know that my motherly task is to lead you all to Heaven. Open your hearts, allow God to inflame your hearts with the flame of His love and mercy. Be children of the light; be prayerful, be humble, be obedient and you will shine brighter than the sun. Others will come to know that you are God's children. Pray, pray, pray! Thank you for listening to my message.

Message from Our Mother of Compassion and Love
January 18, 1993, 7:45 a.m.

Dear children, greetings to all! I am grateful for your coming to spend time in prayer.

My dear children, today, I invite you to continue to decide for God and put Him first in your lives; in this way you will be helping me to lead you all to my Son.

I am Your Mother Come from Heaven to Love You

Message from January 18, 1993 (Continued)

I love you, dear children, and you must believe that I am here helping you to decide for your own conversion. Pray to God that He may send you His peace, that you may share it with others. Pray children, pray, for only through prayer do you obtain the answers to your prayers.

My little ones, you will never understand the important role that you play in God's divine plan. Only through prayer will you begin to comprehend God's salvation plan for humanity. God is calling you to His peace, to His love, to His grace. Pray that your hearts will be open to God's invitation to live in His grace. God's grace is an invitation for you to repent and to be converted. So pray, pray, pray! Thank you for listening to my message.

Message from Our Mother of Compassion and Love
January 28, 1993, 8:50 a.m.

Dear children, greetings to all! I, your heavenly Mother, thank you for your commitment to being here.

My dear ones, today, I call you like never before to take my messages of prayer and conversion seriously. I am here, my children, to teach you how to love God with your heart and soul. Do not allow Satan to distract you from living my messages.

My children, be thankful to God for His love and mercy. Be open to all His blessings and share His blessings with your loved ones. God is with each one of you, and He listens to all your prayers, so pray with faith and confidence.

Message from January 28, 1993 (Continued)

My children, pray with your family and cultivate their hearts with your prayers. Your family is so special to God, and each of your loved ones is a gift from God. Love your family and pray with them. In this way Satan will not be able to touch you or separate you from God, for where there is love and prayer, Satan will not enter or dwell. So pray and love one another. I love you, my children. Thank you for listening to my message.

Message from Our Mother of Compassion and Love
February 2, 1993, 8:20 a.m.

My Dear children, greetings to each one! I, your heavenly Mother, thank you deeply for gathering here for prayer. God's blessings are with you and with your families.

My dear children, today, I invite you again to decide for God. Desire only to be converted and to return back to the love of God. You should not have any other goal, but to live the Gospel and share the Gospel with others.

My children, you must remember, there is no other way that you can go to Heaven if you are not reconciled back to God. So again, I say to you, be converted, and pray, pray, pray!

My children, ask God to inflame your heart and soul with His flame of love. Open your hearts, open your hearts, and allow God to possess your everything. Allow Him that created you to be the Master of your lives, allow Him to be your everything. If you do this, my children, Satan cannot distract you from doing the Will of God. When you allow God to possess your everything, God lives in you, and you in Him. I love you all. Thank you for listening to my message.

I am Your Mother Come from Heaven to Love You

Message from Our Mother of Compassion and Love
February 8, 1993, 7:15 a.m.

My Dearest children, greetings to each one! I, your heavenly Mother, thank you with deep gratitude for coming together to pray the Rosary. Know that God blesses all your efforts.

My little ones, today, I call you to prayer of the heart. When you pray, open your hearts and pray with your heart. Believe in your prayer and do not doubt.

My children, God is loving and merciful, and when you pray He listens to all your prayers. Therefore, open your hearts to God's love and mercy, and He will touch the very depths of your heart and soul.

My children, know that I am with each one of you, loving you and teaching you and leading you to my Son. This, my children, is my motherly task. I ask that you help me to lead you to my Son by living all of my messages that I am giving you. I love you, my children, open your hearts and decide for God and be converted. Peace, my children, peace. Thank you for listening to my message.

I am Your Mother Come from Heaven to Love You

Message from Jesus and Our Mother of Compassion and Love
February 13, 1993, 6:10 a.m.

While I was praying to the Holy Spirit, Jesus and Mary came to me, and the following conversation took place.

Our Lady
Good morning, my daughter! Your prayers are very beautiful; they bring joy to my heart.

Janie
Blessed Mother, please help me with my husband.

Our Lady
Love your husband, love him, love him. I have so many blessings for you and your family, but I cannot give you these blessings until you remain obedient and be a loving and compassionate wife. Ask my Son to inflame your heart with the flame of His love, so that you can be one love, one heart with my Son.

Janie
Blessed Mother, I will do what you ask of me. Can you give me instructions for Sister M.? I do not have any details to what she is asking, but you know. What should I say to her?

Our Lady
Invite her to pray a nine day novena to the Holy Spirit, and at the end of her novena the Holy Spirit will instruct her on what to do.

Janie
Thank you! Could you tell me anything about whether something special will happen in our city, like other cities? Tell me only if it is God's Will that I know.

Our Lady
Yes, my daughter, your city will be a city where many of my children will flock to.

Janie
Is something special going to happen at Saint John Neuman?

Our Lady
Yes! Many blessings will come upon this parish.

Janie
What about New Orleans? Do you have anything that I can share?

Our Lady
Yes, I wish to thank each one of my children for all the wonderful work that they are doing to bring others to my Son. I thank you, I thank all my children with deep gratitude. Continue doing God's work. God will bless you, God will bless you.

Jesus
My daughter, thank you for your obedience, for leaving everything and going out when My Father is calling you to give witness of the teachings you have been instructed to share with others. Know that you do not go alone on this journey, for My beloved Mother and I are always with you where ever you go. Do whatever My Mother instructs you to do. I love you, My little nothing and My little flower.

Janie
Oh Master, I love you; thank you, thank you for coming to visit me this morning. I love you. Do you have anything for New Orleans?

Jesus
Tell My children, that I, too, thank each one of them for loving and honoring My Mother and sharing her love with others. They all have My special blessings for all the work that they are doing to share their love and faith with others. I thank you, all My little humble servants.

I am Your Mother Come from Heaven to Love You

Account of an experience in flight to New Orleans, LA
February 13, 1993, 1:30 p.m.

Today, I arrived in New Orleans. The people that God sent me to stay with are a wonderful family, Mr. and Mrs. S. God blessed their home. Now, I am preparing for Mass and Adoration and then my talk. Praise be to God.

This is an account of my experience on the flight. I saw two angels, dressed in white and a burgundy red. They were huge, and each angel was on each side of the plane and supported the plane as it flew. (This was from Austin to Houston).

Later on, as I took the flight from Houston to New Orleans, I saw four angels dressed in blue and white. On their heads they each had a crown of roses. These angels were huge and beautiful. My angel, Michael, was with me, and we talked, and he shared God's love with me.

Later on after my talk, I was asking Padre Pio to intercede for me, and I asked him if I could be his spiritual child. At this, I saw a vision of a dream I had about four years ago. In this dream I was somewhere out in a field. I was preparing for confession. During this dream I saw two confessionals, and I was going to one of the confessionals, but I heard a voice that came from the other confessional. The voice said, "I will hear your confession, for I know your sins, and your sins are not many."

When I entered this confessional, there was a priest there, who later on I found out was Padre Pio. (I had seen his picture in a book). About a few months later I had another dream. In this dream I was between what appeared to be the Pope and this priest, who was Padre Pio. The Pope was in front of me and Padre Pio was behind. The crowd around me was trying to hurt me, but Padre Pio kept telling me, "Do not be afraid, no harm will come to you."

This was the vision I saw. Then I heard Padre Pio's voice say to me, "You do not have to ask me if you can become my spiritual child, for when you had the first dream, you became my spiritual child.

I am Your Mother Come from Heaven to Love You

Message from Our Mother of Compassion and Love
Mississippi, February 14, 1993, 8:00 p.m.

To my Beloved Priests and Sons,

Prepare, my children, for the Kingdom of the Father. Feed the flock that has been entrusted to you by the Father. Feed them spiritual food, and prepare their souls to live the Gospel. Take your calling as priests seriously, and prepare your own hearts as well, for you will be the strength that will lead your flock in the coming tribulation. So prepare with strong prayer, and know that I, your heavenly Mother, am praying with you and for you.

Message from Our Mother of Compassion and Love
Mississippi, February 14, 1993, 9:45 p.m.

My dear children, I am here to bless each one of you. I am here in a very special way. I want to thank you for all your prayers and sacrifices. I love you all so dearly. Peace, peace, peace!

Message from Our Mother , February 15, 1993

FOURTH ANNIVERSARY OF OUR LADY'S VISITATION TO JANIE

My daughter, my daughter, rejoice, rejoice, for My Son and I rejoice with you! How happy I am, my child, my heart is as joyful as the singing of the birds. My little one, you look to the sky as I speak these words to you, looking to see a sign in the sky. We, my Son and I, are not among the clouds. We are in your heart, your sweet and precious heart. Rejoice, my Son and I are present with you this very moment.

I am Your Mother Come from Heaven to Love You

Message from Our Mother of Compassion and Love
February 18, 1993, 8:20 a.m.

Dear children, greetings to all, and thank you for being here today!

My children, today, I invite you to continue to love one another and to prepare your hearts through means of prayer. Do not talk about prayer, but pray and spend time alone with God.

My children, you live such busy lives, and when you leave your homes, many of you have not even stopped to give thanks to God or ask for His blessing upon your daily activities. How do you expect for God to bless you, when you do not take the time to ask?

Remember, my little ones, the power of prayer: 'Ask and it will be given to you, seek and you will find, knock and the door will be opened.' Know that God's love and mercy is beyond your understanding. Ask God to bless you and He will. He will cover you with His love and peace. So, pray and trust God, trust God. Do not leave your homes without praying.

Oh, my little ones, listen to me! I am trying to teach you the importance of prayer, for prayer opens your heart to receive God's blessing. Pray, pray, pray, and show God your deep gratitude for all His blessings by means of prayer. Thank you for listening to my message.

I am Your Mother Come from Heaven to Love You

Message from Our Mother, February 23, 1993, 7:15 a.m.

Dear children, greetings to all! I thank each one of you for coming together to pray for one another. You have my deep gratitude for all your prayers and sacrifices.

My children, today, I call you to prepare your hearts through much prayer and fasting. Open your hearts and abandon yourselves completely to God and trust in my intercession.

My children, God is calling you to return back to His love and mercy. Do not go on adding more distraction to your lives by ignoring God's calling. Decide for love and return back to God, and He will provide you with all that you need.

My little ones, I invite you, again, to prayer of the heart, where you abandon yourselves to my intercession. Pray, my children, pray. Through prayer your hearts will become pure and holy. Do not have the smallest worry. Am I not here to help you and to guide you?

My children, trust me, and all will go well with you if you listen to my motherly messages. God has allowed me to remain with you for such a long time, but my time with you is short. Please, my children, waste no time and be converted, and decide for God today. Do not wait; God is calling you. I love you, my children, be converted and abandon yourselves completely to God's love and mercy. Thank you for listening to my message.

I am Your Mother Come from Heaven to Love You

Message from Our Mother of Compassion and Love, March 2, 1993

Dear children, today, I invite you to continue to live my messages of prayer, fasting, and conversion. Be loving, and accept one another with unconditional love.

Open your hearts to my motherly love and share my love with your family. Do not have the smallest worry in your hearts, but trust God with all your prayers. Be witnesses of living the Gospel.

My children, many of you are experiencing much suffering in your lives. I am here to help you to turn your suffering into joy by uniting your suffering with my suffering. Offer your suffering for the triumph of my Most Immaculate Heart.

I invite you to pray to the Holy Spirit, that you may be enlightened to do God's Will. Pray each morning, these words:

My heavenly Father, today enlighten me by the Holy Spirit, so that I may offer all that I say and do to Your loving care.

Allow the words of the Holy Spirit to whisper softly in your ears throughout the day:

Your Will, father, only Your Will. Amen.

Thank you for listening to my message.

I am Your Mother Come from Heaven to Love You

Message from Our Mother of Compassion and Love, March 11, 1992

My dear children, greetings to each one! I thank you for all your hard work and the suffering that you have endured. Know, my little ones, that God blesses all your efforts.

My little ones, today, I continue to invite you to prayer of the heart, where you surrender all to God, Who loves you so tenderly. Rejoice, my children, and continue to live my messages by your example. Be a living testimony to others; in this way, you will help me to bring others to conversion.

Prepare yourselves every day with strong prayer, and be loving to all whom God puts in your path. Be obedient, my little ones, and listen to my motherly teachings, for I am here to teach you about the love of God.

If you respond to my requests and put my messages into practice, you won't have to worry about anything, for you will be under my shadow and protection. I will take care of you and your family. I will teach you everything about love and prayer. I will lead you closer to my Son's Heart.

My little children, you must open your hearts and decide for conversion. Learn to love God with all your hearts. Then, the Holy Spirit will enlighten you in all aspects of your lives. Pray, my children, pray. I love you all. Thank you for listening to my message.

Message from Our Mother of Compassion and Love
March 12, 1993

My daughter, before you begin your prayers consecrate yourself to my Sorrowful and Immaculate Heart. My child, I bring you the love of God and all His blessings. Pray for the grace of perseverance, pray with all your heart for your persecutors, and love them like God loves them.

I am Your Mother Come from Heaven to Love You

Message from Our of Compassion and Love
March 13, 1993, 3:00 a.m.

VISITATION OF THE MISSIONARY IMAGE OF OUR LADY OF GUADELOUPE

<u>Our Lady</u>
My child, thank you for staying up and praying with me for all my children throughout the world.

My child, you cannot begin to realize the many graces and blessings that you have received through bringing my tilma to your city. Great blessings are being given to your family and to my son, my beloved priest. As he sleeps, God is showering his heart and soul with many blessings.

My child, this morning I wish to share with you how very much God loves you. He created you, only because He loves you, and His love is eternal. You are precious to Him. Everything about you is so special to God.

<u>Janie</u>
Blessed Mother, why does God love me so much? He knows how sinful I am.

<u>Our Lady</u>
That is why He loves you, because you are a sinner. He blessed you with the gift of free will. You chose to let Him be the Master of your life.

<u>Janie</u>
Blessed Mother, were you speaking of your priest when you told me that your son closed the door to your Immaculate Heart?

<u>Our Lady</u>
Yes, my child. This has pierced my heart so. My sons, the priests, have not yet been able to fully understand that by turning away from my Immaculate Heart, they turn away from my Son.

Many of my beloved wounded sons are living impure lives. Holy Mass has become a routine. My sons are constantly in a hurry and do not spend time in prayer, especially before they celebrate Holy Mass and when they hear my children's confessions. They rush my children that God has put under their guidance.

My sons are so far away from my Son, Jesus. There is so much disobedience in the Church and many of my priests live in darkness. They indulge in drinking, smoking, using profanity, and there is no love between many of my priests.

<u>Janie</u>
Why are you telling me all of this?

<u>Our Lady</u>
My child, this is the time the Church needs much prayer because of their sinfulness. My priests are living in the time of great apostasy. There is so much division and disharmony among my priests. There is little unity in the Church.

This, my child, is what hurts and pierces my Sorrowful Heart. Many of my priests are responsible for my children leaving the Catholic faith. My children are hungry for the love of God, and my priests do not have love in their hearts to love and feed my wounded children.

<u>Janie</u>
What about the priests that do live their vows.

<u>Our Lady</u>
These are my beloved priests who console my Sorrowful and Immaculate Heart. Pray for them, for they suffer much persecution from my other priests who live in disobedience.

<u>Janie</u>
Oh Blessed Mother, it's such a shame to see all this going on in the Church, but I promise I will pray. I promise, I too, will console your Sorrowful and Immaculate Heart.

<u>Our Lady</u>
Thank you, my little one, thank you.

<u>Janie</u>
Blessed Mother, do you want me to go to Mexico to visit your tilma?

Our Lady
My child, I, your true Mother come from Heaven to love you, desire that you and your family make a special trip to Mexico City, while my miracle of the tilma remains untouched or destroyed by human hands. Come, my daughter, and there I will also speak to you of many more of my motherly concerns.

Janie
What is the second part of your message? (Janie had received a private message earlier).

Our Lady
My child, open your heart and listen to my request and my motherly cry. I have come to bring to all my children the love of my divine Son back into their sinful hearts.

I came as Mother of Compassion and Love to lead my children back to God. My motherly task is to put an end to all the massacre of my innocent souls who cry out to God in agony when they are being murdered in their mother's wombs. Those little innocent souls are suffering the death of my Son on the Cross in Calvary. Their Calvary is in their mother's wombs.

Pray, my child, please. I am begging you to pray so that this horrible evil will end. I need all my children's prayers. Together we will put an end to this horrible sin.

My child, if more laws continue to be passed to kill innocent souls, many, many will go to hell. This evil has spread throughout the world like a plague. It has even begun to spread to Mexico City, where this horrible sin had stopped through my apparitions to my son, Juan Diego. Now, many of my children have begun to commit this horrible evil again.

If my children in Mexico City do not heed my request, my tilma will vanish forever.

That is why I am asking my children to turn from this deadly sin, to repent and turn back to God, Who is love. Listen to my message and let it penetrate your heart.

I am Your Mother Come from Heaven to Love You

Message from March 13, 1993 (Continued)

Thank you for your time. God will bless you. God will bless you! Consecrate yourself and your family everyday to my Sorrowful and Immaculate Heart.

Message from Our Mother of Compassion and Love
March 16, 1993, 9:00 a.m.

Dear children, greetings to all! I bring special blessings to each one to thank you for your many prayers and sacrifices. Again, I say, thank you. Through your prayers many of my children are being touched throughout the world. Continue to pray with faith and with love in your hearts.

My children, I ask you to endure your trials and sufferings for the conversion of the many souls who live in darkness. Do not become discouraged when you suffer difficulties in your daily lives, but offer up everything to God, Who knows all your needs.

My little ones, do not forget that I am with you in all your sufferings and in your joys. Believe and trust in my intercession and in my motherly concern for each one of you. Thank you for listening to my message.

I am Your Mother Come from Heaven to Love You

Message from Our Mother of Compassion and Love
March 22, 1993, 9:05 a.m.

Dear children, greetings to all! Thank you for all your many prayers. Know that with each prayer that you say, a divine jewel is added to your crown in Heaven. Rejoice and continue praying with love in your hearts, for this world is in need of much prayer.

My children, today, I am here to tell you to love your family and accept them as God accepts you. Again, I invite you to unconditional love.

Do not become discouraged when your loved ones are weak in their faith, but continue to pray for them and love them, as God loves you when you suffer from lack of faith. Know, my little ones, that only through prayers and love in your heart will you be able to achieve your walk in faith.

Today, I call you to love your family and come together for family prayer. Together as a loving and prayerful family, you will obtain salvation. Together, you will decide for conversion. Love one another and be at peace. Thank you for listening to my message.

I am Your Mother Come from Heaven to Love You

Message from Jesus in the Blessed Sacrament
March 24, 1993, 12:25 a.m.

<u>Jesus</u>
My child, greetings. I, Jesus, your Master and Spiritual Spouse, bring you, My sweet Janie, My love. Do not let anything upset you, not your illness, nothing. Think only of Me, for in Me you will find and have everything.

I, Jesus, your Master, love you My little sinner, like no one else could love you. I know that your suffering has been tremendous, but it is nothing compared to my suffering for love of you. Yes, My love for you is immense.

Let go of all your fears and worries and allow yourself to be loved by Me. Let My love consume you. Come into My Sacred Heart and stay with Me forever. Do not despair, My little wilted, wounded flower; in My love your sweet fragrance of purity will come to live again.

Let Me penetrate every fiber of your being. Open your heart and soul to this great love of Mine. My sweet child, I solemnly tell you that joy will overcome you, and this joy will carry you away into My arms. Allow yourself to be carried in the wings of My love for you. Learn and desire to suffer more, for it is through this suffering that I visit you daily. Yes, My love, in your suffering you meet Me, Jesus, daily. Suffer, suffer with immense pain, for I solemnly tell you that you will find your paradise in your suffering.

My child, I am here with you, and I give you a white rose which represents My love for you. My love, you have pleased Me through all your suffering. Your suffering is heavenly music to all the angels and saints, for through your suffering many souls have decided for conversion.

You please Me, My child. Although you suffer with your illness, you are always giving of yourself to your family and to others. You give without complaining. At night you suffer your physical pains silently. Only I know how you suffer.

Your role as a wife brings joy to My Heart. You give your love to your husband in a special humble manner. Know, My love, that in loving your husband you love Me.

118

Message from Jesus, March 24, 1993 (Continued)

I AM. Your love for your family is so pleasing to Me, that I want you to hear it again and again from Me. Janie, My little flower, the smallest and most humble flower, you are so special to Me. I AM.

I will have the angels inscribe in your heart with letters of gold that have been dipped in My Precious Blood, how special you are to Me and how very much I love you.

Prepare for more suffering and love Me as I love you. Let My love for you be your every breath. Allow My love to be felt with each beating of your heart. I love you, My love. You are Mine. No one will harm you, no one. You are Mine. I AM.

Janie
Jesus, I do feel special! Thank you! I will live and die pleasing You, my Master and my Love. I love you.

I am Your Mother Come from Heaven to Love You

Message from Jesus, March 26, 1993
Ascension Thursday

<u>Jesus</u>
My dear child, welcome to My Eucharistic Heart. Allow your Savior to embrace you in My True Presence at this moment. Rejoice on this day, the feast of My Ascension, which is a day of great joy.

My little flower, how much I love you, and how much I yearn for your complete abandonment. Give all your love to Me; hold nothing back. Be Mine, be Mine. I, your Jesus of Love and Mercy, will deliver you from all your foes. I will protect you from the calamities and pestilence that have invaded the world.

The world is in such darkness, and much prayer is needed due to its sinfulness. Pray with your family and offer your prayers to console My Eucharistic Heart. Abandon your lives totally to Me, your Jesus of Love and Mercy. I AM.

My child, be open to all of My Mother's messages and live them. Be a living witness of Her messages and convey them to others around you. Pray for purity of heart and decide for holiness. I solemnly give you My word that, when the great darkness absorbs the world and its sinfulness, only those with pure hearts will live through this terrible time. There will be much fear for those that have ignored the signs of these times. Many will die in their wretchedness, for they disobeyed My Father's Commandments.

My child, help your own family and teach them about My love and mercy. Bring them closer to My Heart, and My love and mercy will protect them during this terrible darkness.

<u>Janie</u>
My Lord, when will this darkness happen? Is it the Father's Will that I know when?

Message from Jesus, March 26, 1993 (Continued)

Jesus

My child, much of what I am telling you is happening in the world, but many people are blind to the signs that surround them. You are surrounded by horrible sin. The world is reliving the time of Sodom and Gomorra.

To the world, these are My words: repent, repent! Know that you have offended My Father. His hand will come upon the world like a bolt of lightening. For you who have continued to live in sin, it will be too late!

To you who have kept watch of these times and have remained prayerful, you have nothing to fear. To you, I, your Jesus of Love and Mercy, ask that you keep vigilant, praying unceasingly, for no one knows when the hour of great judgment will come. Repent and decide for conversion. Gather your loved ones and pray every day for purity of heart, before it's too late. I, your Jesus of Love and Mercy, invite all to enter into My mercy before it's too late! I AM.

I am Your Mother Come from Heaven to Love You

Message from Our Mother of Compassion and Love
April 1, 1993, 7:00 a.m.

Dear children, greetings to all my beloved ones! I bring you God's peace and joy. Rejoice, my little ones, for God loves you. Rejoice and shout with joy, for you are blessed with God's love.

Today, my children, I call you to take prayer seriously and to begin praying more. Some of you have given up on praying. Never stop praying, for prayer is your strength, prayer brings you peace.

Today, my children, I call you to continue praying for peace beginning in your family, and then pray for world peace. Satan is growing very angry, and his goal is to destroy you and your family..

Be strong, my children, and live my messages. Spend more time in prayer and less time talking about prayer. I am here to help you and to lead you closer to my Son. I call you to more family prayer. I am sad, my little ones, you are not spending enough time with your family. You are too busy with activities and programs that do not include your family.

Come together, my children, and grow together through prayer. Be a loving and prayerful family and build your family foundation by means of prayer. Pray for peace in your family, pray for God's peace in the world. Pray, my children, pray. Thank you for listening to my message.

Message from Our Mother of Compassion and Love
April 6, 1993, 8:00 a.m.

Dear children, today, I invite you to continue to pray for world peace and for peace in your families. God wishes to bless each one of you, my children. Be open and receive God's love and mercy.

I invite each of you to continue to decide for conversion and to ask God to bless you with a pure heart, for when you have a pure heart you have no desire to sin. Sin, my children, is what separates you from God.

I am Your Mother Come from Heaven to Love You

Message from Our Mother, April 6, 1993(Continued)

Be loving, my little ones, and keep your hearts pure through the sacrament of Reconciliation. Know, my little ones, that God's love and mercy is an invitation for you to repent and turn away from sin.

Teach your children about the love of God and teach them how to pray with a faithful heart. You must not forget the importance of family prayer. As a family, my little ones, you receive an abundance of God's blessings, and your bond as a family grows in love and in unity. Pray, pray, pray! Thank you for listening to my message.

Message from Our Mother of Compassion and Love
April 12, 1993

Dear children, rejoice, my dear ones! Rejoice, for my Son has risen! Let your hearts shout with joy for my Son's glorious Resurrection! Praised be God forever and ever.

Today, my children, continue to live this joyful Resurrection and allow this joy to settle in your hearts. Share this glorious joy with others. Be happy, my little ones, for God loves you very much, and He blesses each step that you take. Again, I say, rejoice as all of Heaven rejoices.

My little ones, continue to live in my Son's peace and love, and reach out to one another. Extend this peace and love to your families and your neighbors, your community and to all the world.

My children, only through my Son's peace and love will you be able to survive in this world that is in need of so much peace and love. If only you could begin to understand how important this peace and love is to the world, you would be ready to come together as God's children; but you do not understand, for many of you do not have your hearts open, so you continue to suffer.

Pray, children, and ask God for His wisdom and understanding; then, and only then, will you understand my message. Only through prayer will you come closer to knowing the heart of the Father.

Pray! Live in peace and love. Thank you for listening to my message.

I am Your Mother Come from Heaven to Love You

Message from Our Mother of Compassion and Love
April 22, 1993, 7:00 a.m.

Dear children, today, my little ones, I invite you to continue to cultivate your hearts through your prayers. Pray for peace, pray for love, for this world lacks God's peace and love.

Do not allow yourselves to become distracted by your sufferings, but offer everything to God, and He will bless you and your family.

Many of you, my little ones, are enduring much strong suffering and persecution. Know that these sufferings help you in your purification, for God is calling you to purity.

My children, do not blame God when you endure any suffering, for God does not send you sufferings, but he allows such sufferings to take place in order that He may help you. Again, I ask you not to blame God for your sufferings, but cling to God in all your suffering, and He will help you to turn your suffering into joy. He will see you through everything that brings you pain, for He is a loving and merciful God.

My children, you are in the midst of the purification of the world. God is preparing all His children who are open to His love and mercy. You will see changes in this world that will frighten you, but, I tell you, fear nothing but remain children of the light and allow your light to shine, so that others around you will know that you belong to God.

Remember, fear nothing, but love everyone around you with God's love. Remain close as a family and grow closer together through your prayers. Thank you for listening to my message.

I am Your Mother Come from Heaven to Love You

Message from Our Mother of Compassion and Love
April 27, 1993, 8:30 a.m.

Dear children, today, I invite you to continue to pray for peace in your families and to pray for world peace. Do not become discouraged with all the hatred and the violence in this world, but remain in the spirit of prayer, for Satan continues to declare war against all of God's children.

Do not be afraid, but arm yourselves with strong prayer. Pray your Rosaries with faith and love in your hearts. Through your prayers and your love you will overcome the attacks of the power of darkness.

My children, you are living in a time where you will be rejected by your loved ones and others around you. Continue to be humble and loving, for I am with you in everything, each step of the way. I hold you all close to my bosom, and I protect you through my Sorrowful and Immaculate Heart. Therefore, fear nothing, but pray, pray, pray, and remain faithful to God. Allow nothing to distract you from praying together as a family and praying with your neighbors.

My children, again, I say, remain faithful and pray for peace and love throughout the world. God is calling you to a life of prayer, to conversion, to love one another and to live in God's peace. Continue cultivating and harvesting the Kingdom of God through your prayers. Thank you for listening to my message.

I am Your Mother Come from Heaven to Love You

Message from Our Mother of Compassion and Love
May 3, 1993

Dear children, today, I invite you to continue to pray for love in your hearts. Many of you suffer needlessly, for you have not yet learned to love with God's love. I am here to teach you about God's love and to tell you that a heart that loves God - this heart knows peace, joy and divine trust.

My children, love is your strength, and yet many have not understood the importance of praying for a loving heart. Pray every day for love in your family and throughout the world.

Parents, teach your children to be loving by your examples. Reach out to each family member with love, especially those who have not yet decided to convert. I invite you to begin building Family Cenacles of love and prayer all around you. Begin in your homes, in your church, in your community and throughout the world.

Hurry, my children, do not hesitate! Take my messages to heart and live them. My time with you is short. Live love, today and everyday; then you will begin to see hatred, pride, and jealousy vanish from your hearts.

Remember, my little ones, the teachings of Sacred Scripture concerning love. Love is patient, kind, not conceited or jealous. Love is not selfish, it is not happy with evil or wrong doings. Love is happy with truth, love never gives up. Where there is love, there is faith, hope and patience.

Love is eternal, for love pours out from the Father's heart upon all humanity. His love endures forever. Thank you for listening to my message.

I am Your Mother Come from Heaven to Love You

Message from Saint Michael the Archangel
Thaxcala, Mexico, May 16, 1993

My Little One, I, St. Michael the Archangel, Chief Commander of all the Choirs of Angels, brought you to this holy place to ask you to be obedient and attentive to what I command you to do.

Listen, my little one, listen with your heart. I, St. Michael, command you to awaken the practice of devotion to me, St. Michael and all the choirs of angels, in all hearts through the love and devotion that you have in your heart, and that you practice daily. I, St. Michael, will bestow my perpetual protection over all who will listen to this message of love and devotion to the holy angels. All who listen and put into practice this devotion daily will have perpetual protection from all the nine choirs of angels.

God made the angels for the protection of all of His creation throughout the world. The holy angels have only one desire: to please God by seeing to the safety of His children and to guide all of God's children to complete holiness.

Listen, my little one, and do not resist what I, St. Michael, command you to do. Tell everyone the importance of the devotion to the holy angels, for in the time of great darkness, I, St. Michael, with all my army of angels will protect all who have had a devotion to the holy angels. For this time will be a terrible time of great fear and distress for everyone. Only those souls who have lived in the service of goodness and purity will live through this terrible darkness with the assistance of the angels.

Many, who have resisted to believe in the protection and the intercession of the holy angels, will perish during the time of great darkness, for they have denied the existence of these most holy spirits, the holy angels, and they have failed to believe in God. What a terrible time this will be for these souls without faith. For those souls that practice daily devotion to the holy angels, these souls have the perpetual protection and intercession of all the angels in Heaven throughout their lives.

Again, my little one, do as I command you. Spread devotion to me, St. Michael, and all the angels without hesitation, without delay! Have no fear, for I, St. Michael the Archangel, will protect you as you follow my command. I love you, my little one, I love you, have no fear.

127

I am Your Mother Come from Heaven to Love You

Message from Our Mother of Compassion and Love
May 19, 1993

Dear children, today, I invite you to continue to pray together as a family. Learn to forgive and to love one another.

My children, love settles in your hearts when you are willing to forgive those who have wounded you. Many of you suffer from wounded hearts and from lack of forgiveness.

My children, I invite you to live in God's love. Put all grudges, all hatred aside. In this way the flame of God's love will settle in your hearts. As you learn to forgive, you will begin to experience the heavenly peace and joy that God bestows on those who forgive. Your hearts will blossom like heavenly flowers; your souls will be as pure as a newborn child.

My little ones, pray together as a family everyday. Live in the joy and peace of knowing that God has blessed you and your family. When you unite in family prayer, an abundance of graces are bestowed upon you.

Pray, my children, pray. Forgive others and God will forgive you. Pray the family Rosary every day. The Rosary is your weapon. Satan flees when you pray the Rosary with love and faith. Pray, pray, pray! Thank you for listening to my message.

I am Your Mother Come from Heaven to Love You

Message from Our Mother of Compassion and Love
May 24, 1993

Dear children, today, I invite you to prepare your hearts to receive the gifts and guidance from the Holy Spirit.

Pray with love and faith in your hearts. You will receive all the blessings from Heaven that God will pour out on you through the power of His Holy Spirit.

My children, waste no time on worldly distractions. Decide for conversion! Pray for purity and holiness of heart.

Again, I invite you to pray as a family. Teach your children about the love of God. Guide them towards the road to holiness through your example as parents. Pray for your children and love them. Thank you for listening to my message.

Message from Jesus in the Blessed Sacrament
May 30, 1993

My Child,

Welcome to My Eucharistic Heart. Today, a year ago, you were called to share your teachings on the family with others. God is pleased with your obedience. You, My child, have matured in wisdom and discernment. Through your prayers and sacrifices many families have decided for conversion. Many families pray together through your teachings on family prayer. I thank you deeply.

You have dedicated your life to be in the service of My Father's work. Through your perseverance many souls have been renewed.

My child, you have learned to prepare well before you share with others on the teachings of the family. You pray and you fast and your teachings produce much fruit. You speak with love and peace in your heart, and those who listen to your words experience the love and mercy of God in their hearts. Your teachings move their hearts, so that they want to return back to My Father. You have done well.

Go, therefore, My child, and continue sharing with all My children, near and far, the importance of family unity, prayer, forgiveness and loving one another unconditionally. Live in harmony in My Father's love and peace.

Teach My families that their only goal and desire should be to serve My Father. The only way to obtain this is through purity of heart. A heart that loves My Father has no desire to sin.

I, your Jesus of Love and Mercy, send you, My child, to share the teachings on the family to all who will hear My words. Teach husbands and wives the importance of loving one another, for many have allowed their hearts to grow cold. They must learn to love one another all over again. They must rekindle that love that they once promised to one another, those beautiful marriage vows they spoke before the altar of My Father.

Love and forgiveness must be restored in the family. Only in this way will they be able to live through the great pestilence and calamity that will cause many to perish.

Share this message and continue cultivating and harvesting the hearts of the family. Have no fear; God is pleased with your obedience in this effort. He is pleased.

I am Your Mother Come from Heaven to Love You

Prayer given by Jesus on the eve of Pentecost
May 30, 1993, Evening

FAMILY CONSECRATION TO THE HOLY SPIRIT

Come, Holy Spirit, Our Creator, come to hear us and to prepare our sinful hearts, as we consecrate ourselves, as a family, to you.

Oh, Divine Light, You, Who knows and searches all hearts, receive our family consecration. Unite our hearts with Your flame of love and guide us to live our family consecration, that all we do may be pleasing to God.

Come, Holy Spirit, (on this Your feast day), and inscribe Your love and light in our hearts. Write in our hearts the Commandments and the love of God, that we may live in Your light.

Holy Spirit, knit our souls to You and draw us closer to You. Send the flame of Your love and give us the gift of prayer, that we may pray with our hearts, "Abba, Father, we love You and we praise Your Holy Name."

Come, Holy Spirit, Love of God, accept our family offering, and receive our prayers, which we give to You today.

Come, Holy Light of God, come and make Your dwelling in our family. You, Who are the giver of many gifts, renew our love for You and for one another. Renew our understanding and heal the conflicts that exist in our family, which create distance between us and God.

Come, Holy Fire, and enlighten our hearts with wisdom and discernment, that we may have only one desire: to please God.

Holy Fire, renew in our hearts the wonders of Pentecost and enlighten each family member both present and absent. Let Your love possess our whole being and with

Prayer given by Jesus, May 30, 1993 (Continued)

Your love heal our marriages, our addictions, our unforgiveness and the many problems that exist in our family. Enlighten us and help us to detach from all worldly desires and to make Heaven our goal.
Holy Spirit, be our comforter and Consoler. Rule our lives and with Your love; burn away all our faults. Bring unity to our family. Give us new hearts that are loving and patient, hearts that are generous and charitable, and hearts that have no room for jealousy or evil, loving hearts that desire only God's love and truth.

Come, Holy Spirit, come. Come, Holy Spirit, come, now and forever, come. Amen.

Prayer given by Jesus on, May 30, 1993
Evening, The Eve of Pentecost

FAMILY CONSECRATION TO THE SACRED HEART OF JESUS

Oh Most Sacred Heart of Jesus, we come to You as a family and consecrate ourselves to Your Sacred Heart. Protect us through Your Most Precious Blood and keep us pure and holy.

Oh dear Jesus, we are so far away from Your most pure and Sacred Heart. As a family we need Your help. Heal all the quarrels that exist in our family due to our unforgiveness and lack of love for You. Heal our unbelieving and unconverted hearts and lead us to Your Sacred Heart with love. Unite us as a family and remove all stain of sinfulness from our souls. Help us to be a prayerful and loving family, so that through our example we may lead other souls to Your Most Sacred Heart.

We give you our hearts, dearest Jesus, and consecrate our family through the fourth generation. Through the prayers of our dearest Mother Mary may we live this consecration every day of our lives. Amen.

Most Sacred Heart of Jesus, have mercy on us.

I am Your Mother Come from Heaven to Love You

Prayer given by Our Mother of Compassion and Love
May 30, 1993, Evening

FAMILY CONSECRATION TO THE IMMACULATE HEART OF MARY

Oh Mother Most Pure, we come to You as a family and consecrate ourselves to your Most Immaculate Heart. We come to you as a family and place our trust in your powerful intercession.

Oh dearest Mother Mary, teach us as a mother teaches her children, for our souls are soiled and our prayers are weak because of our sinful hearts. Here we are, dearest Mother, ready to respond to you and follow your way, for your way leads us to the Heart of your Son, Jesus. We are ready to be cleansed and purified.

Come, then, Virgin Most Pure, and embrace us with your motherly mantle. Make our hearts whiter that snow and as pure as a spring of fresh water. Teach us to pray, so that our prayers may become more beautiful than the singing of the birds at the break of dawn.

Dear Mother Mary, we entrust to your Immaculate Heart our hearts, our family and our entire future. Lead us all to our homeland which is Heaven. Amen.

Immaculate Heart of Mary, pray for us.

133

I am Your Mother Come from Heaven to Love You

Message from Jesus in the Blessed Sacrament
May 31, 1993, During Adoration

My Child,

Welcome to My Eucharistic Heart. I, your Jesus of Love and Mercy, thank you for your concern for My beloved brother priests.

My little servant, continue to offer your prayer and fasting for My Vicar, My beloved Pope. Pray for his protection, for he will undergo a great suffering. There is much division within the Church. Many of My brother priests have turned against one another.

The schism continues to grow more and more. The schism feeds on the disobedience in the Church, and the disharmony among My beloved brothers. The schism grows in strength as My brother priests rebel against My Vicar on earth. Pray for the purification of the Church. Pray for My Vicar, pray for him. Support him and love him, as I, Your Jesus, love you.

Message from Our Mother of Compassion and Love
June 3, 1993

Dear children, today, I invite you to continue to unite in family prayer. Many blessings come upon the family that prays together. Offer your family prayers for conversion and for peace in the world.

My children, do not become bored with prayer. You must pray in order to understand the importance of prayer. Prayer is your strength and prayer brings you peace.

Many of you become angry when your prayers are not answered right away. You allow yourselves to become discouraged and you stop praying. Know, my children, that you endanger your soul when you stop praying. Satan takes this opportunity to fill your hearts with more lies. His only goal is to separate you from God and to discourage you from praying at all. So many of today's families have ceased praying, for they have allowed Satan to separate them from God.

I am Your Mother Come from Heaven to Love You

Message from Our Mother , June 3, 1993 (Continued)

Remember, my children, God hears all your prayers. Pray with faith, trusting God. Do not become discouraged, but pray and be converted. There is so much need for prayer in this world that suffers from lack of faith. I love you, my children. I am with you, praying with you and for you. Thank you for listening to my message.

Message from Our Mother of Compassion and Love
June 8, 1993

Dear children, today, I invite you to spend more time adoring my Son. Love one another with forgiveness in your hearts. Learn to forgive all who have caused your hearts to be sorrowful. Unite your suffering with my Immaculate Heart and take refuge. I will help you with all your trials and suffering. Through my Immaculate Heart I will lead you closer to my Son's Heart.

My children, be courageous in your suffering and trust in your prayers. Many of you are experiencing difficult times. Know that I am with you. Again, I say, have courage and faith. I will not abandon you, not even for one moment.

Pray every day to the Holy Spirit to inflame your hearts with His truth and light. Pray for wisdom and guidance in all that you do. God will send His Spirit of Truth.

Love one another, little children, with forgiveness in your hearts. Ask God to send you His love and peace. Be converted! Be converted! Thank you for listening to my message.

I am Your Mother Come from Heaven to Love You

Message from Our Mother of Compassion and Love
June 14, 1993

Dear children, today, I invite you to pray to the Holy Spirit for enlightenment, so that you may be more aware of God's love in your lives.

My children, be living witnesses of the Gospel and be a light to others. Do not become discouraged when you suffer. Pray to God to give you His grace to endure your many difficulties.

My children, love as God's holy family, and be loving to one another. Parents, love your children. Stand by them when they suffer or when they make the wrong choices. These are difficult times for all who are trying to live by God's Commandments. It is extremely difficult for all the young people. Satan is busy trying to destroy them through every temptation possible.

Parents, be patient with your children, as God is patient with you. Much prayer is needed for the family to convert. Satan will not succeed in his plan to destroy you if you pray together as a family. Satan will not enter in the homes of the family where love and prayer is their strength. God's angels protect the homes of the faithful.

Be converted together as God's family. Live in harmony and in love. Pray, pray, pray, and love your children, for they are gifts from Heaven. Thank you for listening to my message.

I am Your Mother Come from Heaven to Love You

Message from Jesus in the Blessed Sacrament
Feast of the Sacred Heart, June 18, 1993

My Dear Children,

My peace be with you, as you listen to My message that I give through My little daughter, whom I speak to, concerning the families in the world. On this day, I, your Jesus of Mercy, bless all families throughout the world. Know, My children, that time is short and soon all apparitions will cease.

Today, I, your Jesus, call each family to come and take refuge in My Sacred Heart. Let My love heal your family quarrels, your marriages. Consecrate your families to My Sacred Heart, and through My love you will be healed. My children, why are your hearts so closed to hearing My warnings, My calling you to repent and to decide for conversion? Haven't you understood My Mother's message to change your hearts and to return back to God? My Mother has called you time and time again through her messages to decide for conversion before it's too late, yet many of you have ignored her request. Now, My children, I, your Jesus, call you to amend your lives and to make reparation for all your sins.

Parents, I speak to you, My beloved: be concerned about the salvation of your children. Teach them to pray and to love themselves. Teach them to be pure. In this way Satan will not cause them to fall into his evil traps. Beloved parents, do not hesitate; protect your children through your prayers. Know that whenever a husband and wife unite in prayer, your prayers reach the throne of My Father immediately, for a good marriage has all the blessings from Heaven.

Pray, My beloved family, pray and consecrate your lives to My Sacred Heart. The family that consecrates their home to My Sacred Heart, there, I make My dwelling. That home is protected by the love of My Sacred Heart, and My graces are poured on this family.

Come to Me, all My beloved families. I speak, also, to My priests and My religious, for you, too, are called to live as a family. Live in My love, in My peace, in My joy, for I am the Way and the Light that leads to salvation.

137

I am Your Mother Come from Heaven to Love You

Message from Our Mother of Compassion and Love
Feast of the Immaculate Heart of Mary, June 18, 1993

Dear children, the peace of my Son be with you, and may His love open your hearts as you listen to my message to the families. Listen to my message, my children, and listen with your hearts. I, your heavenly Mother, have come to bring new words from Heaven. I have come to teach you about the love and mercy of my beloved Son, Jesus. Only by repenting and turning away from your sins will you come to know His love and mercy.

In order to repent, you must look into your souls; in this way you will come to understand the sinfulness that lies within your souls. You will see the things that attach you to this world. Listen, my children, to the words of your heavenly Mother; be reconciled back to God. Repent and amend your lives by making reparation for your many sins. Open your hearts, for now is the time of mercy, when my Son's mercy is being poured out on all mankind. Consecrate yourselves and your children to my Immaculate Heart, and with my motherly mantle I will protect you from my adversary and see to your safety.

My beloved children, live as God's family, loving and forgiving one another. To my beloved husbands, love your wives and bring them closer to my Immaculate Heart through your prayers. Be strong in your faith and provide the spiritual needs of your family. Do not waste precious time involved in activities which do not bring unity and love to your family. Pray to St. Joseph, to help you to be that heavenly husband, loving your family and being patient with them.

My beloved husbands, I speak to you, for God made you the head of your family, as my Son is the head of the Church. Listen, and embrace your wives and your children with God's love. Do not be afraid or embarrassed to be humble, to be loving, to be gentle, to be forgiving, and to be patient, for these are the virtues of heavenly husband.

To my beloved wives, listen to your husbands, be submissive and love them with God's love.

Little children, obey your parents, love them, and pray for them.

138

I am Your Mother Come from Heaven to Love You

Message from Our Mother, June 18, 1993

Take refuge in my Immaculate Heart, for I am the gate that leads you to my Son. I am your Mother, who has come from Heaven to love you and to teach you as God's family. Thank you for listening to my message.

Message from Jesus in the Blessed Sacrament
June 18, 1993

My Dear Child,

Welcome to My Sacred Heart. Come and take refuge in the One Who loves you the most. Let your heart be consumed with the flame of My love. Think about nothing, only be with Me, your Divine King. Embrace this moment of My presence and allow yourself to be loved by My love. Open your heart, My little precious one, open your heart, for tonight I desire to give you graces beyond your understanding.

When you come to Me, I will soothe your aching heart with My love. I will melt away everything that worries you with My love. My love will heal you, My love will refresh you. You will realize that I am your everything; you need nothing else when you are with Me. I love you, My little one, and I desire to love you until you are completely consumed by My love. Come take refuge in My Sacred Heart. Come and be with the One Who loves you more than anyone else. Be silent, be at peace, only feel My love.

I am Your Mother Come from Heaven to Love You

Message from Our Mother of Compassion and Love
June 24, 1993

Dear children, today, I invite you and your family to abandon yourselves completely to my Son's love and mercy.

Pray, children, so that your lives may become a continuous prayer, so that through your prayers peace will reign in many hearts.

Pray every day to the Holy Spirit, that He may enlighten you in all your efforts. Teach your children about God's love. Teach them about my motherly intercession, so that they may consecrate their lives to my Immaculate Heart. I will protect them and guide them with filial love.

Do not grow tired of prayer, for prayer brings you peace. Continue praying as a family, trusting God with your prayers. Live by faith and love, praying in reparation for the sins of the world. Thank you for listening to my message.

Message from Our Mother of Compassion and Love
July 5, 1993

Dear children, today, I invite you to pray for a loving heart. Ask my Son to inflame your heart with His love, so that you may love others with His love.

My children, many of you are suffering and you wonder why God allows you to suffer. He allows you to suffer to draw you closer to Him. Much suffering is due to lack of love and forgiveness and not knowing my Son.

I beg you, dear children, to spend more time with my Son. He will teach you to love, for He is love. My little ones, when you have a loving heart, forgiveness comes easy. When you forgive, you bring joy to others whom you have wounded. Please pray for all the suffering in the world.

My children, be more united as a family. Do not waste precious time! God is calling you to repent and to amend your lives before it's too late!

Message from Our Mother, July 5, 1993 (Continued)

Please do not take one another for granted. Do not abuse one another through your lack of kindness. You live together as a family, yet you are not aware of one another's presence. You have alienated yourselves through your busy schedules.

My children, you have no time for family prayer. This pierces my Immaculate Heart. Dear children, put all programs aside. Come to know one another. Love one another and allow God's love to bless you as a family. Thank you for listening to my message.

Message from Our Mother of Compassion and Love
July 15, 1993

Dear children, today, I invite you to continue to pray and fast for your own conversion and for the conversion of the world.

My children, I thank and praise God for the time that He has allowed me to be with you, and to draw you closer to Him.

My little ones, many of you are suffering and feeling unloved by your family. You are feeling lonely, and you have experienced much anger towards your family.

I invite you to pray and fast, and you will discover God's love, which will help you to accept your family with a loving heart. He will give you the grace to endure all your suffering. Know, my children, that my Son was rejected by His family.

I invite you to rejoice and to open your hearts to God, Who loves you with unconditional love. Allow His love to penetrate your hearts, that you, too, may love with God's love. Thank you for listening to my message.

I am Your Mother Come from Heaven to Love You

Message from Our Mother of Compassion and Love
July 20, 1993

Dear children, today, I invite you to trust God with all your prayers. My dear ones, I know that there is much difficulty and suffering in your family. Know that these are difficult times, and much prayer is needed throughout the world.

Satan is very active in trying to destroy all of God's children. Do not have the smallest worry or fear, for I, your heavenly Mother, am with each one of you. I protect all my children through my motherly mantle.

Take refuge in my Son's Sacred Heart and in my Most Immaculate Heart, for in the Two United Hearts you will find your safety. Every day, consecrate your lives to the Two Hearts and no harm will come to you as a family.

Pray and fast for the conversion of the world and for peace. My little ones, pray to the Holy Spirit to enlighten your hearts, so that you may understand the value of prayer and fasting. Know that they are inseparable.

My children, God will give you the grace to pray and fast. All you have to do is ask Him. Learn to pray and fast, so that you may overcome all the natural disasters, calamities, and pestilence that surround you.

Trust in my intercession, for I am interceding for all your needs. Thank you for listening to my message.

I am Your Mother Come from Heaven to Love You

Message from Our Mother of Compassion and Love
July 26, 1993

Dear children, today, I invite you to continue to live my messages and decide for conversion. Open your hearts to God's blessings. Live in God's peace and put all doubts, worries and anxieties aside. Do not waste precious time talking about prayer, but pray with faith in your hearts. Live my messages and be witnesses of living my messages. Share my messages with others.

My children, God loves you very much. This is a time of great mercy. God is calling all His children to turn from their sins and to convert. Repent and be converted, be converted! Pray together with your family. Pray the Rosary every day! Thank you for listening to my message.

I am Your Mother Come from Heaven to Love You

Message from Jesus in the Blessed Sacrament
July 29, 1993, 9:30 p.m.

Jesus
My beloved child, I send you to My beloved families to share My love and My mercy with them. Speak to them about the importance of family prayer and family love. Invite them to return back to My Eucharistic Heart and allow My love and mercy to melt away their faults and their sinfulness. Share with them that in Me, they will find and know peace like never before, for My heart is gentle and My peace will inflame their hearts with the fire of My love, the love that is perpetual. Share with My beloved families how they wound My Sacred Heart, when they do not put their trust in Me.

Janie
Jesus, would You give the families a message?

Jesus
To the husbands and wives, I, Jesus, invite you to renew your marriage vows and to allow Me to help you live in perfect love and peace with each other by consecrating your love for one another to Me. If you respond to My invitation, your homes will be homes of joy and love where prayer will be your strength, for you will be focused on doing My Father's Will. Your children will shine like the stars in Heaven through their obedience and purity. I will provide all that they need until they reach Heaven. Hear My voice, My beloved families, for I, your Jesus of Love and Mercy, speak to all who hear Me. Turn away from your sins and turn back to My Father Who loves you.

As My beloved Mother tells you to listen to her Son, so I, your Jesus of Love and Mercy, tell you to listen to My Mother. Live her messages; decide for conversion before it's too late. Listen, My beloved families, hear My words: love one another, forgive so that you may be forgiven. Come to Me and bring Me all your concerns, and I will make you whole. Do not be afraid or worried about your struggles, your needs and your difficulties. Put your trust in Me, your Jesus, Who loves you and waits for you with a loving Heart.

I am Your Mother Come from Heaven to Love You

Message, July 29, 1993 (Continued)

Janie
Thank You Jesus, thank You. My Beloved Mother, do you have anything to add to your Son's message?

Our Lady
To my beloved children, listen to the calling of my Son and do as He asks of you. Trust Him and love Him. Allow Him to reign in your homes. Consecrate your marriages and your children to His Sacred Heart and my Immaculate Heart and live in God's peace, live in God's peace. Thank you for listening to my message.

Message from Our Mother of Compassion and Love
August 5, 1993

Dear children, today, I invite you to continue to pray for peace in your family and for world peace.

My children, offer all your prayers and sacrifices for my beloved Pope, for his journey to visit with the youth on the feast of my glorious Assumption. God will send His blessings and graces throughout the United States through the visitation of my beloved Pope.

Pray for his protection and for this holy gathering, asking St. Michael and all his angels to protect his visit to the United States.

My children, continue to consecrate your family to my Son's Sacred Heart and to my Most Immaculate Heart. Let Our Hearts be your family refuge. Love one another and live in God's peace.

Pray to the Holy Spirit for enlightenment and to guide your daily walk to purity and holiness. Pray your family Rosary and accept one another as God accepts you.

My children, do not allow yourselves to be distracted from your prayer time. God nourishes your souls through your prayers. Spend time with my Son in the Blessed Sacrament. He will give you His peace, that you need so much to do God's Holy Will.

I am Your Mother Come from Heaven to Love You

Message from Our Mother, August 5, 1993 (Continued)

My children, my time with you is short. Live my messages. Do not fear or become distracted with all the natural disasters, the calamities, and the pestilence that sweeps the world, but pray and fast. These are the signs of the times when you need to repent and amend your lives. Prepare for the triumph of my Most Immaculate Heart. Listen to my message, listen with your hearts. Live my messages. Thank you for listening to my message.

Message from Our Mother of Compassion and Love
August 10, 1993

Dear children, today, I invite you to pray and fast with a deeper commitment for the intentions of the Two United Hearts. Remain steadfast, my children, allowing nothing to distract you from praying and doing God's Will.

My children, do not be sad through the difficulties that you are enduring. Know that these are the signs of the time, when you will suffer much.

You will be rejected, ridiculed. Many will say that you are not in tune with the reality around you. Your loved ones will make it difficult for you to pray, and they will accuse you of praying too much.

You will experience these sufferings and much more. Remember, you are under my shadow and motherly protection. No harm will come to you. Your heavenly Mother will protect all her children.

Remain loving, prayerful, and obedient to living my messages. Allow yourselves to endure all your crosses for the intentions of the Two United Hearts. You will not go wrong in this effort.

Pray for my beloved Pope and show your gratitude to God by means of prayer, for allowing His Son's Vicar to visit the United States.

Message from Our Mother, August 10, 1993 (Continued)

I tell you, my children, God is blessing you through my beloved Pope's visit. He is truly chosen by God to be His Son's Vicar on earth. Pray for him, pray for him. Continue to pray with your family every day. Do not allow any distractions to keep you from prayer time. Thank you for listening to my message.

I am Your Mother Come from Heaven to Love You

Message from Our Mother of Compassion and Love
Feast of the Assumption, Elgin, Texas, August 15, 1993

Dear children, today, I, your heavenly Mother, bring you heavenly blessings. Rejoice, my children, and unite your joy with all of Heaven on this glorious day.

Today, I pour out my motherly blessings to all my children throughout the world. Open your hearts and embrace your heavenly Mother who loves you dearly.

Take refuge in my Most Immaculate Heart and trust in my intercession. Live my messages every day! Do not allow any distraction to keep you from walking towards the path of purity that I traced out for you. Continue to pray and fast with a deeper commitment for peace in the world. Pray for the souls most distant from my Son, Jesus.

My children, do not become bored with prayer and fasting. Know that through prayer and fasting many souls discover God, and the fruits of your prayer and fasting is their conversion. Prayer and fasting purifies your own heart.

Listen to your heavenly Mother and help me to lead you to my Son, Who loves you more than you could ever understand. Turn from your sins and be converted, be converted!

My children, I want to extend my gratitude for all the suffering and difficulties that you endured for my beloved Pope. Through your prayers and sacrifices you dissolved many of Satan's evil tricks. Your efforts protected my beloved Pope. Again, I extend my deep gratitude. God will bless you, God will bless you!

My children, continue to look towards my Immaculate Heart, consecrating everything to me. Know that I present all your needs to my Son, Jesus. He is pouring His love and mercy to all of mankind.

I invite you to enter into His love and mercy and be reconciled back to God. Love one another, and allow your love to penetrate everyone you meet. Rejoice, and let your joy move you to embrace your family and the world around you. Thank you for listening to my message.

I am Your Mother Come from Heaven to Love You

Teaching from St. Joseph, August 24, 1993, 6:00 a.m.

My Little One,

I St. Joseph, ask that you prepare your heart and hear with your heart my words and my guidance for your family. I will speak to you about the virtues of a husband, the wife and children. Listen to my words and write them down, so that you may share what I tell you with others.

You asked what should a husband be to God and his family, and what are his responsibilities? Write what I tell you: God, Himself, assigned the husband as the head of his family. The husband is charged with complete responsibility over his family.

These are the virtues of a husband: that he is chaste, giving his love to no other woman but his wife. He must pray for purity, so that he remains pure in his thoughts and desires. He must be meek and pray for humility, so that he may be gentle and loving. He must pray for the virtue of obedience, so that he may persevere with love and faith in doing all that is required of him as a husband. These are the virtues that will assist the husband in his daily walk with God and with his family.

The husband has the responsibilities to his family that a priest has to his church. A priest is called to leave everything and to be one with God. A husband is called to be one with his wife. A priest takes his vows of chastity, poverty and obedience at the time when the Church ordains him; the husband takes the vows of purity, chastity and obedience at the time of his marriage. A priest is given responsibility over his church: to pray and nurture his flock and to guide them closer to God. A husband must do the same with his family.

A husband must look towards God to send him His Holy Spirit for strength and guidance. He must pray for wisdom and discernment, in order that he may stay on God's level path that leads towards Heaven. A husband should be gentle and loving. He should provide the necessary needs of his family. He must be loving and firm in the discipline of the children. A husband must look to God and to his family for strength and support.

149

I am Your Mother Come from Heaven to Love You

Teaching from St. Joseph, August 24, 1993 (Continued)

<u>Janie</u>
The husband has a lot of responsibility!

<u>St. Joseph</u>
Yes, the husband plays the most important role in his family for God looks to him to take care of his family, to love his wife with gentleness and tenderness and be to be a model for his children, especially his sons. The role of the husband is to love his wife and his family like Christ loves the Church.

The prayers and love of both husband and wife produce much yield in the lives of their children, for the children are the fruits of their love.

The role of the wife is to trust and submit to her husband, to assist him in his role as head of the family. She must love her husband with gentleness and tenderness, giving herself totally to him and no one else. The wife must bring all decisions to the husband's attention, so that together they decide what's best for the family. The place of the wife is at home, to be there for her husband and her children. A wife must accept her role as a mother and wife. She must be humble, loving and gentle towards her family.

A wife must pray, so that she may not be distracted from the role assigned to her by God. She must pray for strength, so that she won't become bored with her responsibilities as a wife.

A wife's most precious treasures, besides God, should be her family. She must treasure her husband's love and stand by him at all times. Her love will give her husband strength.

A wife is precious in God's eyes. Through her love for God and her spouse she brings forth life, the birth of her children, God's gift from Heaven, the fruit of their love. Wives are special to God; they are beautiful roses that blossom as they bring forth life. The virtues that a wife must pray for: purity, obedience and humility.

The role of the children is to be obedient to their parents and to follow the teaching of their parents. Children must remain pure and chaste, concentrating only on what pertains to them concerning their well being. They must pray for wisdom and discernment in choosing their friends. They must assist their parents in daily responsibilities.

Teaching from St. Joseph, August 24, 1993 (Continued)

They must study hard, putting their trust in God with their education. Children must pray for protection, asking Most Holy Mary to keep them under her motherly protection. Children must love and respect themselves, their parents and others.

Children must not be anxious with choosing careers, but they should pray and listen to what God is asking of them. They should remain chaste and pure and not fall into temptation with the opposite sex. Children must allow themselves to be children and not be anxious about growing up. Children should be joyful, enjoying their childhood and allowing the love and prayers of their parents to help them in their journey.

My little one, I have given you guidance to help you understand the role of the family. Trust in my intercession and pray for all families, so that through your prayers God will bless the families in the world. You have been entrusted with the mission of the family. Continue to trust Jesus and Most Holy Mary in all your prayers and sufferings.

This will be a difficult school year for all children. Consecrate this school year to my intercession, and I will protect all children, for the temptations will be strong. The evil one will attempt to destroy many through drugs, fornication and unhealthy relationships. Pray for your children, pray for your children. A family must pray together every day and love one another.

I am Your Mother Come from Heaven to Love You

Message from Our Mother f Compassion and Love
August 26, 1993, 8:30 a.m.

Dear children, today, I invite you to continue to trust in my intercession. Do not become discouraged with your sufferings and disappointments. I know, my children, that you are being rejected and that you are suffering much persecution. Do not worry or fear my little ones, for God is pouring out His blessings on you. He is guiding you through the narrow path that leads to Heaven.

Rejoice my children, and endure all your crosses with joy. Let nothing distract you, but look to my Immaculate Heart and trust in my intercession.

My children, I invite you to spend time in prayer and to read Holy Scripture. I ask you to pray to God to send you His Holy Spirit, that you may be able to imitate the teachings of the Gospel: to live without fear or worry. Remember you are like salt that gives flavor to the world through your prayer. Do not allow your prayers to become weak through all the distractions around you. Allow your light, which is your faith, to shine, shine, shine!

My children, remember that I am with you, and that I present all your petitions to my Son, Jesus. Allow me to help you to be pure and humble. Continue to pray with your family, and teach other families to come together for prayer. Pray your family Rosary daily and abandon yourselves to God, Who knows all your needs.

I love you, my little ones, and I am with each one of you. Never forget this. Thank you for listening to my message.

I am Your Mother Come from Heaven to Love You

Message from Our Mother f Compassion and Love
August 31, 1993, 8:20 a.m.

Dear children, today, I thank you for all your prayers and sacrifices. Continue to endure your trials and sufferings without complaining, for I am with you each step of the way.

Continue walking toward the path of holiness and purity that I have traced out for you. Pray with your family, and be more committed to praying the Rosary together. The Rosary, my little ones, is your weapon. Through praying the Rosary, you disarm Satan and dissolve all the temptations that he puts in your path.

My children, I ask that you pray to my most chaste spouse, St. Joseph, who is an example to all through his obedience and humility. He remained faithful to God through all trials and tribulations. He looked toward God with filial trust. Nothing distracted him, for he knew that God would not abandon him. I invite you, my children, to allow Saint Joseph to be your model and to trust in his intercession.

My children, live in peace and be joyful, allowing nothing to frighten you. God is pouring out his blessings on you. Allow your faith to be your strength and your love to be your foundation. I love you my children. I love you all and I am with you. Thank you for listening to my message.

I am Your Mother Come from Heaven to Love You

Message from St. Joseph in the Prayer room
In the Prayer room, September 1, 1993

My Little One,

I, St. Joseph, have come to say thank you for sharing the message that I gave you (message given on 8-24-93) with others. Write these words quickly:

To all who read and accept this message with your hearts: these souls will receive great blessings from God, the Almighty Father. God will bless them in such a way and inflame their hearts with His love, that they will have the desire to convert. They will hunger for the love of God, and they will be able to forgive their family and to love them with God's love.

Share this message without delay! Thank you my little one.

I am Your Mother Come from Heaven to Love You

Prayer to St. Joseph inspired by the Holy Spirit
September 1, 1993

PRAYER TO ST. JOSEPH

Oh most chaste pure spouse of Most Holy Mary, Holy Guardian of the Most Holy Family and guardian of all families, pray for us.

Most holy St. Joseph, I come to you and beseech you with all the ardor of my heart and soul, to listen to my prayer. I commend myself, my family, and all families in the world to you.

Hear my prayer, oh most pure and humble Foster Father of our Savior, and intercede for all families in the world.

Most pure St. Joseph, God entrusted you with complete charge over the Savior of the World and the Queen of Heaven. You provided for them with tender, loving care, until you were called by God

I, your daughter (son), ask that you take complete charge over me and my family. Intercede for us before the throne of the Most High God, for I know in my heart, that God will hear your prayer as you intercede for us. He will not deny you anything for you never said no to God, but you responded with your heart and soul with a total yes.

I love you, my beloved St. Joseph, I love you. Help us to be pure, humble and obedient. Amen.

I am Your Mother Come from Heaven to Love You

Message from Our Mother of Compassion and Love
September 6, 1993, 7:20 a.m.

Dear Children, Today, I invite you to continue to allow God's love and peace to penetrate your hearts. Allow yourselves to be guided through the Holy Spirit, and abandon yourselves completely to the love and mercy of God.

My little ones, offer your prayers and sacrifices for peace in the world. Take refuge in the Sacred Heart of my Son, Jesus, and in my Most Immaculate Heart, for your safety lies within the Two United Hearts.

My children, learn to live without fear or worry, imitating every word of Holy Scripture, for God is calling you to complete trust in Him. Continue to pray with your family and allow God's blessings to penetrate your heart and share God's blessings with others.

My children, I want to thank you; so many of you have matured in your love for God and for one another. You have grown in wisdom through your constant prayers and sacrifices. God will bless you and reward all your efforts.

My children, embrace your crosses with joy. Live as God's pure instruments, imitating God's love and peace.

I love you, my little ones, I love you. Remain joyful and loving. Pray for God's love and mercy, for the essence of the heart of the Father is love, and mercy is His fruit. Thank you for listening to my message.

I am Your Mother Come from Heaven to Love You

Message from Our Mother of Compassion and Love
September 14, 1993, 6:55 p.m.
Triumph of The Cross, New Orleans, Louisiana

Dear children, I, your heavenly Mother, extend my gratitude for all your prayers and sacrifices. Through your hard work, many will receive special graces and blessings.

I invite you, my children, to continue to pray together for the conversion of the world, where so many souls continue to live in darkness. Your prayers and sacrifices bring joy to my Immaculate Heart. You have consoled my heart through all your efforts. I love you, my little children, I love you. Peace, peace. Thank you for listening to my message.

Message from Our Lady of Sorrows
September 15, 1993, 12:20 a.m.
During Perpetual Adoration

My Child,

I, your heavenly and Sorrowful Mother, ask that you continue making reparation for the unconverted. Many of my children continue to reject me as their Mother. They blaspheme against my virginity and spread evil rumors against my holy name. This grieves my Son for the rejection that His Mother receives. Many are the offenses committed against my virginity. Many of my children are embarrassed to claim me as their Mother. This rejection causes me much sorrow.

Many are the sorrows that fill my Immaculate Heart, but your being here, visiting my Son, consoles my Sorrowful Heart. Tonight, on the eve of Our Lady of Sorrows, pray with me to stop the horrible evil that has spread like an epidemic throughout the world: the massacre of innocent little souls. This pierces the Heart of my Son and my Immaculate Heart. Pray my child and make reparation for this horrible evil, asking God to forgive this terrible sin.

I am Your Mother Come from Heaven to Love You

Message from Our Mother of Compassion and Love
September 15, 1993, 7:00 p.m.
Feast of Our Lady of Sorrows, New Orleans, Louisiana

My dear children, I, your heavenly Mother, wish to thank each one of you for this beautiful prayer gathering.

To my beloved priests, to you I thank you with deep gratitude for feeding and nurturing the flock entrusted to your care. Continue leading all my children toward the path of holiness. My beloved priests and my children, through this gathering here tonight, you have turned my Seven Sorrows into joy. You, my dear children, have consoled my Sorrowful Heart.

To my beloved daughters (the religious sisters), thank you for coming tonight. Continue, my beloved daughters, to live in purity and in obedience looking to your Spouse, my beloved Son, Jesus. In Him you have everything. Trust Him and love Him, for His Heart overflows with love and mercy for each one of you.

To my children, thank you, thank you! God will bless all your efforts. Continue to pray. Continue to love one another. I love you all, my children, I love you all. Know that each one of you have received special blessings for you and your family. I, your heavenly Mother, bless you all. Peace, peace, peace.

I am Your Mother Come from Heaven to Love You

Message from Jesus, September 15, 1993, 12:30 a.m.
During Perpetual Adoration
Feast of Our Lady of Sorrows, New Orleans, Louisiana

My Child,

Welcome to My Eucharistic Heart. Allow My love to penetrate your soul. Come and journey with Me, and I will teach you how to love with My love. Surrender everything to Me and think about nothing else, for this time that you come to be with Me is precious. Look at My Eucharistic Heart.

(At this time Janie saw rays of light coming out of His Heart).

See how much love I have to give all who come. Let Me love you totally, so that you in turn may love others. Feel the fire of My love. Come, open your heart and soul to My Eucharistic Love.

I remain here for you day and night, hoping that in your busy schedule, you will find time for Me. When you come, I delight with joy and I embrace you with My love immediately. I soothe your tired and aching heart. I refresh you completely and fill you with My love, so that you can go and share My love. I want nothing to come from your heart except My love. I want you to think love, feel love and be love. I want you to be completely Mine, heart and soul.

My precious flower, don't forget what I am telling you tonight. I only desire to love you and every one of My children who come to visit Me during Adoration. Share My words, share My love. Invite everyone to come and be loved by your Jesus of Love and Mercy.

I am Your Mother Come from Heaven to Love You

Message from Our Mother of Compassion and Love
September 16, 1993, 7:35 a.m.

Dear children, today, I invite you to offer up all your prayers for world peace. My children, abandon yourselves completely to my Son, Jesus. Be open to His love and mercy and put your trust in Him.

My little ones, open up your hearts and allow God's love to inflame your hearts. Turn to God and decide for conversion. Turn away from your sins and listen to the calling of God to repent. Do not ignore God's invitation to amend your lives, before it's too late!

My children, allow your heavenly Mother to help you to be pure, to be obedient and to be humble. Pray for simplicity and live simple lives, praying and making reparation for the conversion of the world. Abandon yourselves to my Immaculate Heart and detach from the material world that distracts you from being totally united to my Son, Jesus.

My children, I desire that you be in Heaven with me; that is why I beg you to listen to your heavenly Mother. Listen to me: the world has nothing to offer you. Open your hearts, my children, and decide to live in God's eternal glory. In Heaven, my little ones, you will be happy. You will be completely filled with the love and joy of God.

Come, my little ones, allow your heavenly Mother to lead you and your family to my Son. He will lead you to the Father where you will have complete eternal happiness. I love you, my children, I love you all. Thank you for listening to my message.

I am Your Mother Come from Heaven to Love You

Message from Our Mother of Compassion and Love
September 21, 1993, 10:15 a.m.

Dear children, today, I invite you to live my messages like never before. So many of my children have continued to ignore my messages. Consecrate your families to my Immaculate Heart and remain under my motherly protection.

Pray my children, pray, for Satan is busy destroying families throughout the world. Be strong as a family and pray together every day. My children, do not leave your homes without praying, and do not go to bed without giving thanks to God for all of His blessings. Begin your day with prayer and end your day with prayer. My children, prayer and forgiveness are the keys to Heaven.

Allow God to take charge over your lives, for only through complete abandonment to God will you be able to live through the great tribulation.

My children, take the message given by St. Joseph seriously and do not ignore it. You will receive special blessings in living St. Joseph's message. Pray, asking St. Joseph to protect your family. Consecrate yourselves and your children to him every day, for he is the protector of all families. I love you, my little ones, I love you. Thank you for listening to my message.

I am Your Mother Come from Heaven to Love You

Message from Our Mother of Compassion and Love
September 22, 1993, 8:00 a.m.

Our Lady
I, your heavenly Mother, come to ask a special request of you and your family. I desire that you and your family pray for three months, beginning in the tenth month. I ask you to pray and fasting in reparation and for the coming of the new year, for it will be a year with great suffering.

This new year marks a time when the world will suffer with much calamity and pestilence. There will be more earth quakes and many other natural disasters that will cause the economy to suffer much.

Janie
(I saw volcanoes, tornadoes, earthquakes, floods, etc.)

Our Lady
Many will be left homeless and many will die. There will be much political struggle and world leaders will make unstable decisions that will cause the people to suffer.

Janie
Blessed Mother, this sounds serious.

Our Lady
Yes, my child, many will die from this horrible disease that continues to take millions of lives. (She was referring to aids). This deadly disease is the result of the disobedience of many who live their lives indulging in fornication and committing adultery.

This disease will claim the lives of millions of young children, because of the sins of their parents. Young people will continue having children out of wedlock. Much violence and evilness will grow in the hearts of the young people, for their parents have not taken the time to teach them about God.

My beloved Pope will continue to suffer much for the many sins of the Church. Many of my beloved priests will grow weak in their love for God.

Message from Our Mother September 22, 1993 (Continued)

Janie

(I saw that the Pope would suffer much, perhaps in a physical sense. I understood that the aids virus would become more serious and millions would die from this virus).

Our Lady

My child, this coming year will be a serious year with much suffering. The family will suffer much for their lack of disobedience to teaching their children about the love and mercy of God. Pray unceasingly for these intentions for the next three months. I, your heavenly Mother, will be praying with you and your family.

Message from Our Lord Jesus, September 22, 1993, 1:30 p.m.

Jesus

My beloved one, do not be concerned with My Mother's requests to you and your family. Abandon yourselves to her requests, for truly I, your Jesus, tell you, that this coming year is marked with much suffering and disaster, for the world has not heeded the cry of My heavenly Mother to turn from their sins and be converted.

All that My Mother told you will come to pass and only serious prayer and fasting can lessen these sufferings. I, your Jesus, solemnly tell you, that unless the world hears the words of My heavenly Mother to convert, the world will only know total chaos.

Janie

Jesus, how many earthquakes will come?

Jesus

Do not be concerned with numbers, but turn quickly towards prayer and plead My Father's mercy. My child, many people are prideful and arrogant, these souls will be the ones who will suffer the most. Many will die in their sins.

I am Your Mother Come from Heaven to Love You

Message from Jesus, September 22, 1993 (Continued)

The world lives in darkness, for it will not commit to following the road that leads to holiness. They have ignored My Mother's requests.

My beloved one, hear with your heart My words. Pray for My brother priests and for My Vicar on earth. Pray especially for your country and plead for My mercy before it's too late!

Pray to your guardian angels, for these obedient ones will help you to pray more for these intentions; they will protect you. Pray to the angel that is the protector of your country.

Message from Our Mother of Compassion and Love
September 27, 1993, 8:05 a.m.

Dear children, peace my little ones, peace. Today, I invite you and your family to live in God's total peace, allowing nothing to distract you. My children, purify your lives through means of prayer. Teach your children how to pray, especially in times of difficulty, for Satan is trying to destroy your children.

My dear children, again, I ask that you consecrate your family to my Immaculate Heart. The family that is consecrated to my Immaculate Heart is under my motherly mantle. I see to their spiritual and material needs. Your problems become my problems, your concerns, my concerns. I am with you everywhere you go. I am constantly interceding for you and helping you to obtain holiness and purity. I will dwell in your homes and at your jobs. I will be with your children and protect them while they are away from home. Trust me, my children, and consecrate your family to my Immaculate Heart. Thank you for listening to my message.

I am Your Mother Come from Heaven to Love You

Message from Our Mother of Compassion and Love
October 7, 1993, 8:45 a.m.

Dear children, today, I invite you to decide for holiness and purity of heart. Open up your hearts, my little children, and live my messages. Be living witnesses of the Gospel and share your joy with others.

My children, my time with you is short. Please listen to me and live my messages. Decide for conversion and lead others to conversion. Pray your Rosary every day and teach others how to pray the Rosary. Remember, my children, the Rosary is your weapon. Satan hates the Rosary, for he is aware that through the Rosary he is disarmed.

My children, there is so much sin in the world. Many of my children are not living my messages. Many have turned their backs on my Son. Please, my children, pray and decide for conversion, before it is too late! I beg you, my little ones, do not continue to offend my Son. He is already much offended. Pray the Rosary, pray the Rosary every day! Today, I bless each one present here, and I bless all your families. Be at peace and love one another. Thank you for listening to my message.

I am Your Mother Come from Heaven to Love You

Message from Jesus in the Blessed Sacrament
October 11, 1993, 7:45 a.m.

To My Children attending the Detroit Marian Conference,

I, your Jesus of Love and Mercy, have brought you here to bless you and to fill your hearts with My merciful love. Open your hearts, My little children, and accept all the blessings and graces that you will receive while you are attending this conference. Give Me your fears, all your worries and your anxieties. Give Me everything. Trust Me, your loving and merciful Savior, and abandon yourselves totally to Me.

My little children, I wait for you with My loving Heart. I will speak to you through all My children that were invited to this conference. Prepare your hearts for great graces and blessings. Many of you have come with broken and wounded hearts. I am here to heal you and to answer your prayers. Blessings will be poured out on your families back home. You have come here hurting; you will leave here rejoicing and praising My Father in Heaven. I will flood your hearts with My love and My peace. You will return to your homes with a new heart and loving attitude. All I ask is that you trust Me.

My Heart lies open for you. Come, enter into My Heart and live in My love. Listen with your hearts to all that is said here. Dismiss all doubts, for I solemnly tell you that I, your Jesus, am here with you in everyone of you. This conference is part of My Mother's network, her plan for conversion in the world.

Pray for all Marian conferences throughout the world, so that through your prayers and sacrifices, My Mother's plan for conversion will be manifested. I, your Jesus, bless each one present here. My peace I give to you, My peace I give to you. I love you, My little children, and I am with you always until the end of time.

I am Your Mother Come from Heaven to Love You

Message from Our Mother of Compassion and Love
October 12, 1993, 6:45 a.m.

Dear children, today, I invite you to open your hearts to my Son and decide for conversion. Do not delay, for every second that you waste endangers your soul. Quickly, my children, enter into my Immaculate Heart, which is the gate that will lead you to my Son. Do not procrastinate in your decision, but enter into my Son's mercy and be converted before it's too late!

My little ones, you have entered into a time when you are surrounded by violence, unbelief and much suffering. Know my little ones, that these are the signs of my times. You will see many unpleasant changes in the Church, in the families, and throughout the world. Be wise my children, and prepare your hearts and your families for the reign of my Immaculate Heart through prayer and fasting.

My children, open your hearts and live my messages. Be diligent in praying your family Rosary every day. Remember, prayer opens up your hearts and prayer brings you peace. Pray, pray, pray. Thank you for listening to my message.

Message from Our Mother of Compassion and Love
October 18, 1993, 5:25 a.m.

Dear children, today, I, your heavenly Mother, invite you to continue to pray your family Rosary every day. Pray for all families in the world, especially the families which are most distant from my Son, Jesus. My dear ones, open your hearts and look to my Immaculate Heart for safety and protection. Each day I am bringing you closer to God.

Dear children, I ask that you pray and fast for all my priests. Embrace my priests with the same love that you embrace my Son, Jesus. So many of my beloved priests are suffering and being persecuted for the sake of my Son. Offer up all your prayers and sacrifices for my beloved priests.

167

I am Your Mother Come from Heaven to Love You

Message from October 18, 1993 (Continued)

Please, my children, do not resist my request but be obedient to your heavenly Mother. Pray especially for my beloved Pope, for he is my Son's Vicar on earth. Pray, my children, pray for my priests, pray for my priests. Thank you for listening to my message.

Message from Jesus in the Blessed Sacrament
October 23, 1993, 9:30 p.m.
Eucharistic Marian Conference, Detroit, Michigan

To the Youth

Janie
My beloved Jesus, please give me guidance on what to say to the youth. I am tired and distracted. Tell me what to say. (Jesus said that each person who reads this message should insert their name no matter what their age, for we are all His children).

Jesus
My dear children, to you I, your Jesus, invite you to come and be My friend, and I will be your friend. You and I will begin a friendship that will help you to understand Me and to know Me. My Name is a name that will be so impressed in your hearts.

You see, My little friend, I, Jesus, know everything about you. I knew you before you were born. I have loved you all your life. I know all about your secrets that you dare not share with others. I know about your shyness and the desire that you have in your hearts concerning your future.

Let Me help you to decide about your future, for in Me you will know consolation. I will help you to trust and to love Me. Do not worry, My little friend, I won't tell anyone what you share with Me. I will introduce you to My Mother and you will learn to trust her. She, too, will help you with your decisions concerning your future. I tell you, you don't need drugs, today's music or friends that will mislead you. You only need to know Me.

Let Me be your friend, let Me help you. Come spend time with Me.

Love, Your Friend, Jesus

I am Your Mother Come from Heaven to Love You

Message from Our Mother of Compassion and Love
October 28, 1993, 8:30 a.m.

Dear children, today, I call you to allow your lives to become lives of prayer. Allow the mercy of my Son, Jesus, to settle in your hearts.

My children, be witnesses of living my messages, so that through living my messages, you may be protected by my motherly mantle.

My little ones, allow God to be the center of your lives and faith to be your foundation. Read Sacred Scripture every day and be examples of the Gospel. Listen to my calling to return back to my Son, Jesus, and to enter into His merciful Heart and be converted. Gather as a family every day and pray the Rosary. Do not allow one day to go by without praying together as a family.

My children, do not become bored with prayer. Through prayer you draw closer to God and to holiness. Teach your children the importance of prayer, so that they, too, will come to know my Son in a personal way.

My children, do not forget to ask St. Joseph to assist you to be models of the Holy Family. He will assist your family in every aspect of your lives. He will intercede for your family. Trust in his intercession.

My children, again, I ask that you pray for my beloved Pope and for all my priests. Come, my children, take refuge in the Sacred Heart of Jesus and in my Most Immaculate Heart. Do not fear anything around you, but live in the Two Hearts and praise God, praise God for His love and mercy. Thank you for listening to my message.

I am Your Mother Come from Heaven to Love You

Teaching from St. Joseph, October 29, 1993, 10:25 a.m.

St. Joseph
My little one, be at peace with yourself, for I know that it is hard for you to believe that you are being visited by me. Know, my little one, that you have found favor with God, and that He is pleased with all your efforts.

Tonight, I, St. Joseph, want to teach you about love. First of all, I want to tell you that it is important to pray to God for a loving heart. You must make love the center of your life, for through love you will overcome all evil. Families must allow love to rule over their homes.

The word love is vanishing from the families of today. Evil has taken control of many hearts, and the world is infested with violence and hate. Children are killing children, and the parents have lost control of them. The only attraction that the young people have is to that which is evil. The young find pleasure in fornication, in drug abuse, in music and in relationships that lead to destruction.

The parents have lost interest in their children's well-being. Each day that goes by millions of young people die of unnatural causes. The parents have forgotten their responsibility to their children. Families have forgotten how to love one another.

Janie
Oh, St. Joseph, this is hard, I really feel bad hearing all of this.

St. Joseph
My little one, it is important that the family comes to an awakening and assumes its responsibility to love one another and to allow God to assist them to be a family again.

Do not close your heart to what I, St. Joseph, tell you, but pray for your family and for all families. Share what I, St. Joseph, teach you. The families are in danger, and the power of Satan is strong. He is destroying families everywhere through the power of adultery and divorce.

170

I am Your Mother Come from Heaven to Love You

Teaching from St. Joseph, October 29, 1993 (Continued)

Families must return back to God and ask for His forgiveness and mercy. God's love is eternal, and this world is in much need of His love. Pray for love. Be at peace and be loving to everybody, beginning in your home.

Janie
I love you St. Joseph, thank you.

Message from Our Mother of Compassion and Love
November 2, 1993, 8:15 a.m.

The following conversation was private dialogue between Janie and Our Lady. Janie was directed by Fr. Bordeaux to share this message.

Our Lady
Greetings, my child, how are you this beautiful morning?

Janie
My Lady, I am not doing very well. I have concerns in my heart.

Our Lady
Tell your Mother about them. That is why I am here, to help you and to guide you. Tell me what I can do to help you.

Janie
My dear Mother, I am concerned about people worrying that they need to move and sell their homes to go to safety. I don't know what to tell them, for you haven't asked my family to move to safety and to sell our home. These people believe that they need to buy vehicles and be one hour away from the city. Please help me. This is causing me to be distracted from your teachings and the teachings of Sacred Scripture.

I am Your Mother Come from Heaven to Love You

Message from Our Mother November 2, 1993 (Continued)

<u>Our Lady</u>
My child, I am here to guide all my children to complete holiness. My children must take refuge in my Most Immaculate Heart for their safety. I will protect all my children who take refuge in my Immaculate Heart and who trust in my intercession. My children will not fear anything if they live my messages.

I invite all my children to consecrate their family to my Immaculate Heart and live this consecration every day.

I invite my children to be examples of the Gospel and to live by faith, trusting in the teaching of the Church.

I invite all my children to pray for and support my beloved Pope and to follow all his instructions concerning the teachings of the Church.

I invite all my children not to become distracted by the teachings of the world but to love and follow my beloved Pope.

If my children listen to my messages and live them, they won't fear anything. Again, I say to my children, take refuge in my Most Immaculate Heart and trust in my intercession. I will protect all my children at all times, for they are under my motherly mantle.

<u>Janie</u>
Thank you, my dear Mother.

<u>Our Lady</u>
Be at peace, my child, be at peace.

I am Your Mother Come from Heaven to Love You

Message from Our Mother of Compassion and Love
November 2, 1993, 8:25 a.m.

Dear children, today, I invite you and your family to continue to be witnesses of living my messages. Share my messages with others who live in darkness. Pray for your own conversion and for the conversion of the world.

Dear children, abandon yourselves completely to doing the Will of God. Live the Ten Commandments, for these are the guidelines given by God to His servant Moses. If you follow and live by the Ten Commandments, you will learn to live without fear.

I invite you to spend more time in prayer and less time talking about prayer. Spend time with my Son in the Blessed Sacrament and tell Him all your concerns. Trust in the Presence of my Son in the Blessed Sacrament. The more you visit the Blessed Sacrament, the more your lives will begin to change. You will hunger for and seek holiness, instead of sin.

My little ones, open your hearts and listen to my motherly teaching and follow the path that leads to holiness and purity of heart.

Pray for the Poor Souls in Purgatory and offer up your masses for their intention, for they so long to be in Heaven.

My children, attend daily Mass whenever possible. Invite your children to spend time before the Blessed Sacrament and help them to know my Son. Many parents attend daily Mass and spend time with my Son, but they do not bring their children. Teach your children about God, before it's too late! Pray together as a family. Thank you for listening to my message.

I am Your Mother Come from Heaven to Love You

Teaching from St. Joseph, November 5, 1993, 8:45 p.m.

<u>St. Joseph</u>
Greetings, my little one!

<u>Janie</u>
Good evening, my beloved St. Joseph. It is so good to see you and to have you visit my heart. Thank you for coming to visit me. I am ready and my heart is ready to listen to your teaching and guidance. What will you tell me tonight? Speak, beloved St. Joseph, for I am anxious to hear what you have to say.

<u>St. Joseph</u>
Very well, my little one. Write down what I tell you. Tonight, I will continue to teach you about the importance of love. You see, my little one, love conquers all evil. When God created the world, He created everything with such perfect love. He created the entire human race with such tenderness, with such design to live and exist in His love.

God provided everything for His creation to live in perfect harmony. Nothing was lacking when He breathed life into His first son, Adam. Adam was made into the likeness of God. God was pleased with Adam, and He had such love for Adam, that before Adam came into being, God had provided a perfect paradise for Adam.

Upon seeing Adam's loneliness, God created a suitable partner for Adam. Out of Adam's rib came into existence Eve, the first woman. God was pleased with them and blessed them by telling them to be fruitful and multiply.

God loved them so much that He gave them free will. He only asked one thing of them: not to eat from the forbidden fruit. They disobeyed by the power of temptation, and they turned towards sin and away from God's love. Then sin entered every heart and the entire human race has been living in sin. God has continued to pour out His love throughout time, providing every opportunity for humanity to live in His love and to turn from sin.

174

I am Your Mother Come from Heaven to Love You

Teaching from St. Joseph, November 5, 1993 (Continued)

God in His love and mercy sent His only begotten Son into a world of sin. This Son took the form of a slave and came in the form of an infant to bring God's love back into a world living in darkness. God's Son came as the Savior to redeem the world and to teach humanity to love one another and to live in God's peace. Once again humanity ignores God's love and puts to death the Savior of the world.

Janie
St. Joseph, will God get tired of helping us?

St. Joseph
Never, for His love is eternal to whomever responds to His love. These souls will have peace in their hearts.

I want to help you and your family to learn how to love with God's love. Go forth and share His love by your example. Love is the key to eternal happiness. Pray for a loving heart. Pray for love in the world. You have God's blessings.

I am Your Mother Come from Heaven to Love You

Message from Our Mother of Compassion and Love
November 8, 1993, 8:30 a.m.

Dear children, today, I invite you to pray for my special intentions, so that through your prayers my plan for conversion will be manifested. I invite all families to consecrate their lives to my Immaculate Heart and to pray their family Rosary for the triumph of my Immaculate Heart. I invite all my children to pray and fast for their own conversion and to put God first in their lives.

Pray, my children, and ask God for a prayerful spirit and do not become bored with prayer. Teach your children about the power of prayer and help them to pray. Teach your children about the True Presence of my Son during Holy Mass. There is so much distraction and lack of respect among the youth during Mass, and this saddens my heart. Spend time teaching your children about the Ten Commandments and the importance of living by the Ten Commandments.

My children, listen to my motherly teaching and do all that I ask of you. God has blessed the world through my apparitions, but all is coming to an end. The day is coming when all you will have is my motherly teachings. Many of you will have to learn to live by faith and trust in God. Live my messages and allow me to help you to draw closer to God. Thank you for listening to my message.

I am Your Mother Come from Heaven to Love You

Teaching from St. Joseph, November 12, 1993, 9:30 p.m.

<u>St. Joseph</u>
My child, write down what I, St. Joseph, tell you. Tonight, I want to talk to you about family prayer and its importance. Every family must dedicate at least one hour to praying together.

The family should have an area designated for prayer time, where there are no distractions. Together, the family will begin to grow in virtue and in holiness, as they pray together.

The family must decide for conversion and make Jesus Christ the center of their lives. All family members, young and old, must participate in daily family prayer.

<u>Janie</u>
St. Joseph, what prayers should a family pray together?

<u>St. Joseph</u>
Whatever needs they have as a family. Every family member must learn prayer of the heart, where the family abandons themselves totally to God. They must trust God and seek His mercy in their prayers. The family that includes the Rosary as part of their daily prayer, this family will receive graces and blessings in every aspect of their life.

Through praying the family Rosary, conversion will begin to blossom in the hearts of the family members who are walking in darkness. Through praying the Rosary, God will send His peace and light. Hearts will be healed and love will be born in the hearts of the family. The Rosary is a prayer in which God invites us, through the Holy Spirit, to live the life and mystery of Jesus through the eyes of His Mother, Mary.

I, St. Joseph, ask you, my little one, to share this message. All families must pray the Rosary, trusting Most Holy Mary to guide them gently to her Son, Jesus, as they pray the Holy Rosary.

I am Your Mother Come from Heaven to Love You

Teaching from St. Joseph, November 12, 1993 (Continued)

My little one, invite all families, every one, to trust in the powerful intercession of the Immaculate Heart of Mary. Invite all families to allow Most Holy Mary to teach them how to pray as a family, for she is the perfect example of prayer. She will be present to all who recite the Holy Rosary. As the family gathers for prayer, they must pray to the Holy Spirit to enlighten their hearts.

My little one, to you, I, St. Joseph, extend my gratitude for your patience in writing down all that I share with you. I love you, my little one.

Janie
St. Joseph, I do have one question.

St. Joseph
Tell me, my little one, what is your question?

Janie
Why do you use the word 'must'? Isn't this a strong word?

St. Joseph
My little one, look at the darkness around you. These are troubled times. All must pray and beg for God's mercy. All must be reconciled back to God. Prayer is the answer to this sinful world. Through prayer God sends His peace. Special graces and blessings are obtained through prayer. Now do you understand why I, St. Joseph, tell you that all must pray?

Janie
Yes, it is clear to me why it is a "must" to pray. Thank you, beloved St. Joseph. Thank you.

St. Joseph
Thank you for your patience. God's favor rests on you.

I am Your Mother Come from Heaven to Love You

Message from Our Mother of Compassion and Love
November 18, 1993, 4:45 a.m.

Dear children, today, I invite you to live in God's love and in His peace. Extend His love and peace to others around you. Pray together and love one another with God's love.

My children, I invite you, again, to spend more time together as a family. Many of you have such busy schedules, and you don't have time to be a family or have time to pray together. My little ones, without prayer you cannot come to know God. You must pray, so that God will shower His blessings and graces upon you and your family. Prayer is the tool that will disarm Satan, who is forever busy trying to destroy you. He has only one goal and that is to separate you from God.

My children, open your hearts to my motherly teaching and guidance. You are becoming distracted from prayer, and you are not living my messages. Pray and fast, and you will obtain the answers to all of your family needs. God wants to bless you and to help you, but your hearts are so distracted. Trust in God and abandon your hearts to Him. Be apostles of His love and live Sacred Scripture. In this way others will know that you are children of the light.

Trust, also, in my Most Immaculate Heart and allow me to help you to obtain holiness and purity. Know that I protect all my children who take refuge in my Immaculate Heart. Again, I invite you to take time from your busy schedules and pray together as a family; pray especially the Holy Rosary. Do not allow your children to watch endless hours of television. Spend time together and engage in other family activities which draw you closer to God.

Parents, to you, I invite you to take your vocations as parents seriously and provide for the spiritual needs of your children. So many parents are not aware of how much they neglect the spiritual needs of their children, and this saddens my heart. If more parents would take the time to teach their children how to pray, the violence and disrespect in the family would decrease. Pray, children, pray; time is short. Live my messages and God will bless you. Thank you for listening to my message.

I am Your Mother Come from Heaven to Love You

Teaching from St. Joseph, November 19, 1993, 9:10 p.m.

St. Joseph
Tonight, my little one, I, St. Joseph, want you to ask me any question that you may have on your mind.

Janie
St. Joseph, maybe you could help me and give me guidance on how spouses can strengthen their relationships and how they can renew their love for one another. So many spouses are so distant from one another. Please give me guidance in this area.

St. Joseph
My little one, this is a delicate area and requires much attention. Write down what I tell you.

The reason that relationships grow weak between spouses is that they quickly forget their promises to one another: "to love one another all the days of their lives, in good times and bad times, for better or worse, in sickness and in health." Spouses are happy the first years of their marriage, and they exist in their love for one another. But, soon, they become distracted with the worldly attractions around them. They begin to spend more time apart. They get so involved in their careers and spend less time together. Spouses stop telling each other, "I love you." They alienate themselves from one another through their careers and many other distractions. This causes their relationships to grow weak.

Secondly, they begin their lives together without prayer. God is not present in their lives. Their marriage is not protected, because they lack the power of God's love which is found through prayer. Spouses must make God part of their lives by putting God first in their lives. A day should not go by without spouses telling one another, "I love you."

Spouses should always be lovers, best friends, and special to one another. They should keep their love and relationship fresh and pure through prayer. They should demonstrate their love for one another by doing special things, like showering one another with little gifts and surprises, no matter how small the gift or surprise is. What is important, is that they do it out of love for one another. Spouses should make time to spend with one another, away from all other distractions.

180

Teaching from St. Joseph, November 19, 1993 (Continued)

Prayer and love can make any relationship stay fresh and pure. Spouses can live in God's total bliss, if they put their trust in God and pray that God will bless their relationship. Remember, all things are possible with God. He, alone, can restore any relationship between spouses, but they must pray and put their trust in God.

So, next time someone comes to you with this problem concerning their relationships, remember prayer, trust in God, allowing God to be part of their lives and their love for one another; these are the ingredients to a God-filled relationship. Did this help you?

Janie
Yes, thank you, St. Joseph. Please pray for my family and all families in the world.

St. Joseph
I will intercede for all who invoke my intercession. Good night, my little one. You are favored by God. You have God's blessing.

Janie
Good night and thank you.

I am Your Mother Come from Heaven to Love You

Message from Our Mother of Compassion and Love
November 23, 1993, 8:15 a.m.

Dear children, today, I thank you for all your prayers and sacrifices. Know, my children, that already, many souls are drawing closer to My Son through your prayers.

My children, I invite you to continue praying and fasting for peace in your families and for world peace.

My little ones, be thankful for all the blessings and graces that you receive from your heavenly Father. In just a few days, the Church everywhere will be giving thanks to God for all His blessings. I invite you to take this opportunity to be charitable and share your blessings with others. Feed my hungry children, clothe them, give them shelter, see to their well-being by helping them in every way possible. Pray to the Holy Spirit to enlighten your heart and to inflame your hearts with the gift of charity and with the gift of love.

My children, open your hearts and see with the eyes of your soul, then you will be able to see all the needs that surround you. God calls you to imitate the Good Samaritan in the Gospel and to be charitable and to love your neighbor. Be obedient and share your blessings with others.

My children, today, I invite you in a special way to love my beloved priests. Treat them with respect and love them. Do not mistreat my beloved priests; already, they are mistreated by the unbelievers.

Do not say anything against them, and do not judge them, for God alone is their judge. Love my beloved priests and pray for them, for they are my Son's representatives on earth. They are God's voice and God's chosen ones. Thank you for listening to my message.

I am Your Mother Come from Heaven to Love You

Teaching from St. Joseph, November 26, 1993, 9:30 p.m.

<u>St. Joseph</u>
Good evening, my little one, thank you for preparing for our visit.

<u>Janie</u>
Good evening, my beloved St. Joseph. I'm so glad that you are here. Thank you, thank you. St. Joseph, I'm sorry, but I invited my family to be with me during this visit. I won't have much private time with you, because I also have company.

<u>St. Joseph</u>
Do not be concerned with anything. I, St. Joseph, will help you to be attentive. Are you ready to visit with me?

<u>Janie</u>
Yes, I am.

<u>St. Joseph</u>
My little one, you are sad. Do you want to talk about it? I am here to help you. What is it that is causing you so much sadness?

<u>Janie</u>
I am sad, because I am having problems with being loving towards my family. I am running short on patience, and I feel frustrated. My family and I are in need of much prayer. We have been rude to one another, and my family seems to be bored with coming together for prayer time. This is what's causing me to be sad, because I know that God has blessed our family. It hurts me when we have family quarrels and don't show God our gratitude. Tell me what to do.

<u>St. Joseph</u>
My little one, continue to be strong in your faith and allow God to be your strength. He will give you the strength and love that you need to love your family, especially when you are feeling the way that you are. Pray for your family and keep your focus on your prayers, and not on the quarrels and disagreements. As you continue to pray, God will send you His Holy Spirit to enlighten your heart with His love. You will begin to feel the love that flows from His heart to your heart. You will be illuminated with the love and peace from Heaven. You will be able to embrace your family with God's love.

I am Your Mother Come from Heaven to Love You

Teaching from St. Joseph, November 26, 1993 (Continued)

You must surrender all your feelings of anger and frustration. Empty yourself, my little one, and be filled with the fire and the love of the Holy Spirit. Trust in your prayers for your family and know in your heart that God is listening to your prayers. Never say to yourself, "I don't love my family," but pray:

Dear Father in Heaven, help me to love my family with Your love, for my love is weak.

Remember, my little one, that you were created in the likeness of God's image. He created you out of love, therefore, you must be a vessel of love and love everyone.

<u>Janie</u>
This is beautiful, thank you. I feel the love of God in my heart just hearing you tell me this. I don't feel angry or frustrated with my family. I know in my heart that I can forgive them. I want to be a vessel of God's love always. Thank you, St. Joseph, for this guidance.

St. Joseph, I have a question.

<u>St. Joseph</u>
Tell me, what is your question?

<u>Janie</u>
What about dysfunctional families, those with alcoholism, sexual and physical abuse and other addictions? Sometimes, it is hard to forgive the individual who brings so much pain and shame to the family. It is especially hard when these individuals continue to engage in these behaviors: like the alcoholic who keeps drinking and bringing so much suffering to the family and refuses treatment, the sex offender who continues with his behavior, and the ones who physically abuse others. They, too, continue these behaviors. How does one handle this?

<u>St. Joseph</u>
My little one, love and prayer is the answer to all the sinfulness and disobedience. Only by accepting the love that comes from God will healing take place in many hearts. Only through God's love can this world be healed. Only through prayer will the world know God's peace.

184

I am Your Mother Come from Heaven to Love You

Teaching from St. Joseph, November 26, 1993 (Continued)

When hearts decide to put God first in their lives, then and only then, will forgiveness take place. The pestilence and affliction will decrease and hearts will be made anew. Those afflicted will be healed through the power of God's love and forgiveness. My little one, you must pray and love with God's love. Did this help you?

Janie
Yes, oh yes, thank you!

St. Joseph
Until next week, my little one. Live in God's love and peace. Good night, my little one.

Janie
Good night, my beloved St. Joseph.

I am Your Mother Come from Heaven to Love You

Message from Our Mother of Compassion and Love
November 29, 1993, 8:50 a.m.

Dear children, today, I invite you and your family to prepare your hearts for my Son, Jesus. Open your hearts and pray more as a family. Some of you pray very little.

My little ones, do not become bored with prayer. Know that through praying you obtain many graces and blessings. Do not be overcome with your difficulties and sufferings, but put all your trust in God Who loves you. Trust Him, little children, trust Him. He will see you through all your sufferings.

My children, you must pray, so that through prayer you may overcome your pride and selfishness. Pride and selfishness distract you from being kind and loving. It puts distance between you and God.

My children, I speak to you about pride and selfishness, for many of you are unaware that you suffer from this kind of sin. Many of you are unhappy, and you don't have God's peace, because of your pride and selfishness. Only through prayer and fasting will you overcome all the darkness in your hearts.

Today, I wish to speak to the young. To you, I, your heavenly Mother, invite you to pray more. Put your trust in my Son, Jesus. You are not alone, my little ones. God loves you very much. He wants you to be pure, and to help you and your friends to know Him in a deeper way. I love you, my young children. Pray more with your parents and love them. They need your love and support to help them to be good parents. Pray, pray, pray!

Thank you for listening to my message.

I am Your Mother Come from Heaven to Love You

Teaching from St. Joseph, December 3, 1993, 11:00 p.m.

St. Joseph
Good evening, my little one, it brings joy to my heart to see you happy.

Janie
Good evening, my beloved St. Joseph. Yes, I am happy. I was able to go to Confession and to attend Holy Mass today. This brought joy and happiness to my heart.

St. Joseph
My little one, you have been struggling with doubt in your heart, regarding your experiences from Heaven that God has blessed you with.

Janie
Yes, beloved St. Joseph, I have. It's so hard for me to believe sometimes. No one understands how deeply I suffer from doubt.

St. Joseph
My little one, do not doubt, but believe in your heart that you have found favor with God. He loves you very much.

Janie
Beloved St. Joseph, I am thankful to God, but what can I do for Him? I lack in everything. I have nothing. I am a poor writer, my spelling is bad, I don't know how to talk in large groups. I only do it because I want to please God.

St. Joseph
All that matters, my little one, is that you only desire to please God. By wanting to please Him, you receive all the graces and blessings that you need to do His work. He loves you, because you admit that you have nothing; by saying this you acknowledge your nothingness. This is pleasing to God. You, my little one, are a humble little servant. Do not be distracted with the spirit of doubt, but look at the fruits in your family, and at how much your family is growing closer to God.

I am Your Mother Come from Heaven to Love You

Teaching from St. Joseph, December 3, 1993, 11:00 p.m.

<u>Janie</u>
St. Joseph, it is so good to have you help me to understand myself a little bit better. Thank you! Beloved St. Joseph, would you give me guidance on how we can prepare our hearts for Jesus during this holy season?

<u>St. Joseph</u>
My little one, you prepare through prayer and through the sacrament of Reconciliation. This is a time when you take inventory of the plight of your soul. You evaluate every detail of your life. You bring your sinfulness before the throne of God. This is the time when you ask forgiveness of those around you whom you have injured in some way. This is the time that you reach out to those who have injured you. Through the power of forgiveness love can be born in many hearts, and where there is love, there is peace.

My little one, this is the time when you decorate your heart with purity and holiness, when you prepare your heart to allow the love of the Christ Child to be born in your heart. This is the time to accept the greatest gift of love given to all humanity for the salvation of the world, the greatest gift of love that came in the form of an Infant. The Son of the Most High God is the reason to prepare your hearts and rejoice.

Pray, my little one, that this year many will prepare their hearts to allow Christ the King to be born in their hearts, for God so loved the world that He gave His only begotten Son to redeem the world. This is the greatest gift, the gift of love. Prepare a manger in your heart and allow the Child Jesus to be born in that manger which you prepared for Him.

<u>Janie</u>
Thank you, St Joseph, thank you!

<u>St. Joseph</u>
You are most welcome.

I am Your Mother Come from Heaven to Love You

Teaching from St. Joseph, December 3, 1993 (Continued)

<u>Janie</u>
St. Joseph, will you please listen to this song? It is from me to you.

<u>St. Joseph</u>
Yes, I will listen.

(He listened to the song, St. Joseph, Pray for Me. He smiled).

Live in God's love and peace, my little one. Good night.

<u>Janie</u>
Good night.

Message from Our Mother of Compassion and Love
December 8, 1993, 9:30 a.m.
Feast of the Immaculate Conception

Dear children, today, I, your heavenly Mother, invite you to prepare your hearts for my Son, Jesus. Open your hearts and receive the joy of the nativity of the Infant Jesus. Accept the peace and joy of the birth of my Son, and allow God's blessing to help you to be pure.

Today, on this my feast day of the Immaculate Conception, I invite you to choose the path that leads to purity and holiness.

My children, live in God's peace and extend this peace to others, especially your family. Continue to pray together as a family, preparing your hearts by forgiving one another. Allow this holy season to be a time of peace and joy in your family. Give one another the gift of love which comes from your hearts.

My children, do not allow yourselves to become distracted by material things during the holy season. Do not worry about giving gifts that won't last or feed the soul. Give the gift of love, which costs nothing, but is priceless. Rejoice and prepare your hearts. Allow the birth of my Son to be born in each heart. Thank you for listening to my message.

I am Your Mother Come from Heaven to Love You

Teaching from St. Joseph, December 10, 1993, 9:40 p.m.

St. Joseph
Greetings! How are you my little one?

Janie
Oh, St. Joseph, I am much better now that you are here. Thank you for coming. This is a very special time for me.

St. Joseph
My little one, prepare to write and trust God with the concerns that are troubling you at this moment. God knows what is in your heart. Give Him your suffering.

Janie
Thank you, St. Joseph. Sometimes, it is so hard trying to remain loving and patient in times of suffering, but I will do as you ask of me, for you know our Lord. Please pray for my family and take care of us.

St. Joseph
My little one, trust in my intercession, for I am here to help you and your family. Abandon yourself to God. Give Him your family. Let go, and put all at God's disposal. What would you like for me to help you with tonight?

Janie
St. Joseph, your words have already helped me. I would like for you to teach me about the true meaning of Christmas, and how we must prepare to receive Jesus.

St. Joseph
My little one, Christmas is the most important time of the year. Christmas is a time of joy. It is a time to reflect on the goodness and mercy of God. It is a time of thanksgiving, where all of humanity should open their hearts and be reconciled back to God. It is a time for all the faithful to come and triumph in the glory of God.

Christmas is a time of singing hymns and praises, for the glory of God has manifested in the form of an Infant, Who was born as Savior of the world. This is the greatest gift to all humanity, for God so loved the world that He gave His only begotten Son to the world, so that all would be redeemed through the birth of Christ the King.

I am Your Mother Come from Heaven to Love You

Teaching from St. Joseph, December 10, 1993(Continued)

God chose that His Son be born in a stable to teach the world humility and simplicity, yet many have ignored this message. Christmas is a time of preparing one's heart, a time of reparation for all the sinfulness of the heart and soul.

My little one, in order to understand the meaning of Christmas, one must pray to accept the love of God that was given to the world through the birth of the Infant Jesus in that humble stable. Christmas is a time to reflect on the message given to the shepherds by the angel of God. This message was meant for all humanity. This was the message of God through His angel: "Do not be afraid, for behold, I proclaim to you Good News of great joy that will be for all people. For, today, in the City of David, a Savior has been born for you, Who is the Messiah and Lord. This will be a sign for you; you will find an Infant wrapped in swaddling clothes and lying in a manger."

Suddenly, there was a multitude of heavenly hosts with the angel, praising God and saying, "Glory to God in the Highest and on earth peace to those on whom His favor rests." This is the true meaning of the spirit of Christmas: proclaiming the Good News to all of the birth of Christ the King, and repeating the sounding joy of the wonders of the love of God to all humanity.

Share this message so that all will allow the Child Jesus to be born in their hearts and to share His love and joy with others.

Janie
St. Joseph, this is so beautiful. Just the words and the message of the angel are enough to bring the love of God to all. Thank you.

St. Joseph
Yes, my little one, God gave a message of love to the world through His angel, and this is the meaning of Christmas.

You are welcome. It is late. Prepare to go to bed. Rest in God's peace.

Janie
Thank you, beloved St. Joseph. Thank you!

I am Your Mother Come from Heaven to Love You

Message from Our Mother of Compassion and Love
December 12, 1993, 7:45 p.m.

My Children,

I, your heavenly Mother, thank you for coming to be with me. Thank you so much for the beautiful songs. You, my children, have pleased your Mother through your singing. What a beautiful way to prepare your hearts to receive your Mother!

My children, I know that some of you are suffering, and you are doubting that I am with you. My little ones, I am really here with you. Open your hearts, open your hearts and believe. Do not worry, my children, I will help you in your suffering. Trust in my intercession. Thank you my children, thank you.

Message from Jesus in the Blessed Sacrament
December 13, 1993, 3:15 p.m.

Welcome to My Eucharistic Heart. Come and spend quiet time with Me away from all the distractions of the world. Your being here consoles My Eucharistic Heart.

Today, I, your Jesus of Love and Mercy, invite you to open your heart and receive all My love and peace. My little flower, I am pleased with all your little offerings in reparation for the world.

Today, you have been fasting for My beloved brothers (the priests), and I thank you. Continue to pray and fast, especially for all the priests who are struggling with their faith. Many of My beloved brothers are struggling with the desire of wanting to leave the priesthood. This saddens My Heart, because many priests are being distracted by the world. Because of this distraction, their prayers have become weak.

Many priests do not take the time to pray before celebrating Holy Mass. The celebration of Holy Mass has become routine due to lack of preparation. Many of My brother priests lack the spirit of prayer.

192

Message from Jesus, December 13, 1993 (Continued)

Their hearts and souls have become like dry trees in the winter that lose their life and have become barren with no sign of life in them. Many of My brother priests are dry and barren, for they have stopped loving Me, the Source of their life.

Pray, My little flower, for all My brother priests. Offer your prayers and sacrifices in reparation for their hearts and souls. Through your offerings you will help My beloved brothers to draw closer to Me.

Remember also, My brother priests who remain faithful and obedient to Me in all their sufferings and persecutions, for these suffer the most, for their hearts and souls are united with My Heart. Love and respect all My brother priests and never speak harshly of them, but be noble and help them through your prayers.

My little flower, you have listened patiently to My pain and suffering for My Church. Take this message and share it with others. You have consoled My Eucharistic Heart, and I bless you. Go in My peace and live in My love. I love you, My little flower. Your fragrances are your prayers and sacrifices. Go in My peace.

I am Your Mother Come from Heaven to Love You

Message from Our Mother of Compassion and Love
December 14, 1993, 8:50 a.m.

Dear children, today, I, your heavenly Mother, invite you and your family to prepare your hearts for the birth of my Son.

My children, open your hearts for Him. In this way your hearts will become that humble stable where my Son was born. Allow your lives to become a life of prayer, so that through your prayers many other souls will come to know my Son during this holy season.

My children, I invite you to accept God's love and to live in His love. Do not be distracted with worldly activities, but be concerned about living my messages. Know, my little ones, that when you live my messages, you have nothing to worry about. I, your heavenly Mother, will protect you and your family. Your needs become my needs, your sufferings - my sufferings. I will protect you and you will take me everywhere you go, for you will be under my shadow and protection.

Listen to your heavenly Mother! I want to help you and prepare your hearts for my Son. I want to take you all to Heaven with me, but you must respond to my call and live my messages.

Today, I invite all families to pray a nine day novena in reparation for all my children who do not yet know my Son and in preparation for your own hearts. Offer your novena for the Holy Souls in Purgatory, for on Christmas day many will go to Heaven. Special graces and blessings are given to all humanity on this holy day. Pray, and prepare your hearts. Thank you for listening to my message.

I am Your Mother Come from Heaven to Love You

Teaching from St. Joseph, December 17, 1993, 10:20 p.m.

St. Joseph
Good evening my little one. You are so joyful tonight!

Janie
Yes, my beloved St. Joseph, for God gave me a very special blessing through Father. I am so happy! My heart is full of joy.

St. Joseph
You are very radiant, your heart is filled with God's peace. My little one, what may I help you with tonight?

Janie
Oh, beloved St. Joseph, I am so grateful to God for His blessing and for His priest being obedient to Our Lady by giving me her blessing as she requested. What may I do for all the priests to help them to be better priests?

St. Joseph
My little one, you have a generous heart, and your heart is full of love for priests. Pray for all priests, for these are hard times for the Church. The Church is in the midst of great turmoil. Many priests are struggling with their faith. Priests in great numbers are separating themselves from the Vicar on earth. There is much division in the Church among the priests and religious.

Many priests are not living their priestly vows of poverty, chastity, and obedience. Many priests have separated from God and have lost reverence and love for the Eucharist. The apostasy is growing strong within the Church. Holy priests suffer much because of all the turmoil and the apostasy in today's Church.

Many priests have stopped practicing the sacrament of Reconciliation. Their souls are stained and dark with sinfulness. The world is in need of holy priests that will help guide their people back to God. Many priests alienate themselves from God due to their lack of commitment to follow the true doctrine of the Church. They choose to be part of the world instead of being holy and belonging to God's Kingdom.

I am Your Mother Come from Heaven to Love You

Teaching from St. Joseph, December 17, 1993 (Continued)

Many priests are not feeding the flock entrusted to them, and the flock leaves their shepherd, looking elsewhere to be fed. Many priests have been responsible for their flock leaving the Catholic faith. The Church is in need of much prayer.

My little one, offer up all your sufferings and prayers for the purification of the Church. Pray unceasingly for all priests. Invite others to pray and fast for the Church. Pray and ask the intercession of St. Michael for the protection of the Church.

Share this message, for the Church is in need of purification and conversion. Many priests live in darkness and much prayer is needed for enlightenment of the Holy Spirit. Now, my little one, you know what you must do to help the priests.

Janie
St. Joseph, this saddens my heart, but I'll do as you ask of me, for I know you are the protector of the Church. Please protect all priests, St. Joseph. Thank you. Thank you.

St. Joseph
Good night, my little one. Remain in God's holy peace.

Janie
Thank you St. Joseph. I love you. Pray for us.

196

I am Your Mother Come from Heaven to Love You

Prayer for the Priests inspired by the Holy Spirit
December 17, 1993, 11:00 p.m.

PRAYER FOR PRIESTS

Oh Lord, tonight I pray that you protect every priest under your Heavens. Keep them pure and let them reflect the light of Your Son.

Console Your lonely priests. Enlighten those priests who have lost their way.

Heal Your priests who suffer from woundedness of mind, body and spirit.

Oh Lord, give Your Divine Light to all Your beloved priests who live in darkness.

Bring joy to those priests who are sad and who suffer from depression. Bring Your love and peace to the hearts of all priests.

Oh Lord, God, please do not allow my prayer to go unheard, for Your priests are Your voice on earth. They are Your representatives.

Be merciful and loving toward all Your priests, especially those who have abandoned You. Through Your love and mercy help them to be pure and holy.

Lord, so many of Your priests have helped and guided me. I thank You for these priests.

Lord, this is my prayer for Your priests. Help them and bless them. Let not one of them escape Your love and mercy.

Bring them all to Your Eternal Glory. Amen.

I am Your Mother Come from Heaven to Love You

Message from Our Mother of Compassion and Love
December 20, 1993

SPECIAL BLESSING FROM OUR LADY

Dear Children, Today, I, your heavenly Mother, invite you and your family to open your hearts and receive the gift of love. Rejoice, my children, and abandon your hearts to the love of my Son, Jesus. Trust in my intercession and take refuge in my Most Immaculate Heart. I will protect you, and I will lead you to the Heart of my Son.

My little ones, today I give you my special motherly blessing that you may share this blessing with others. Do not be sad or worried about anything. Let go of everything and know that God loves you. Do not quarrel with one another, for this is a time of joy and peace. Do not allow Satan to distract you from this joy and peace, but trust God with all your prayers like never before. Convert, my children, and receive the light from Heaven and live in this light.

My children, many of you are suffering from loneliness and painful memories. Today, give them all to your heavenly Mother, and trust in my intercession. Today, receive my motherly blessing and never forget this blessing. Share it with everyone. Through my special blessing you will find it easier to convert and to love.

I love you, my children, I love you. Peace and joy, peace and joy. Thank you for listening to my message.

I am Your Mother Come from Heaven to Love You

Message from Jesus in the Blessed Sacrament
December 24, 1993, 10:15 p.m.

Jesus
Welcome, My precious little flower, and thank you for coming to spend time with Me on this special night. You will receive a multitude of blessings while you visit, for it was I, your Eucharistic Savior, Who called you to come to Me.

Janie
Oh Jesus, I know that it couldn't be me who came on my own, especially not knowing if the church would be open. Thank you for this blessed privilege and for blessing me in this way. What is it that I can do for You, my loving Jesus?

Jesus
My humble servant, tonight, I want you to go back into the time when I was born in that humble stable. Journey with Me and see and experience the joy of the Nativity, the gift of love to all humanity.

Janie
Suddenly I am alone, but I can feel God's presence all around me. I am at the stable and I see a small room with friendly animals, which appear to be kneeling. I see a very bright star shining down over this entire region where I am.

It is night, and it's cold. I hear voices singing songs. The language is unknown to me. They are men's voices. I see shepherds a distance from me; they have many flock. A young boy is blowing on his flute and looking towards the shining star. The rest of the men are also looking at the big bright star, and they talk among themselves as if wondering what this big star could mean.

I feel cold, and I am wondering if I should go and warm myself by their fire. (These men have a fire to keep themselves warm). I look back to the stable which is a distance away from me. I begin walking back to the stable and I see our beloved Mother Mary and a multitude of angels cleaning up the stable. St. Joseph is outside gathering what appears to be hay. He puts it around this small area that makes up the stable.

I am Your Mother Come from Heaven to Love You

Message from Jesus, December 24, 1993 (Continued)

All of a sudden, they kneel down and begin to pray and give thanks to God for helping them find a place for the birth to take place. I listen with tears in my eyes, and I begin to pray myself.

The night is clear, and there are numerous stars in the sky. Then all of a sudden, I hear beautiful singing and a loud beautiful voice. I look to see where the voice is coming from, and I see the shepherds illuminated with great light.

I look up to the sky where this beaming bright light is coming from. I see a huge angel with big golden wings. He is dressed in white. His hair comes down to his shoulders. Then I hear him say to the shepherds, "Do not fear! (The shepherds were frightened). I am here with Good News for you, which will bring great joy to all the people. This very day in the City of David, a Savior is born, Who is the Lord and Messiah. You will find a Baby wrapped in swaddling clothes and lying in a manger."

Then a great multitude of angels appeared with the angel, singing praises to God: "Glory to God in the Highest and peace on earth to those on whom His favor rests." The angels left, and the shepherds spoke to one another, saying, "Come, let us go see this Baby which the angel spoke about."

Suddenly, once again I was at the stable. There came a great light from the stable, and I could see the Infant lying in the manger, and Joseph and Mary were next to Him. I felt so much love, that I began to cry with joy. Everyone was in a daze from being surrounded by this love coming from the Infant. What a gift, what a joy! How can God love me so much? Mary and Joseph look so humble kneeling down with their heads bowed down, praying and praising God. Then I am back with Jesus.

Jesus
My child, tonight you have been allowed to witness My birth and My love. Go My child and share My love with the rest of the world. Never forget what you saw here tonight.

I am Your Mother Come from Heaven to Love You

Message from Jesus, December 24, 1993 (Continued)

<u>Janie</u>
Thank you Jesus. I am not quite sure how I will share this, for no one will believe me.

<u>Jesus</u>
Do not worry, but share My love with others. Peace is My gift to you. Merry Christmas, My child. I love you.

Teaching from St. Joseph, December 24, 1993, 11:10 p.m.

<u>St. Joseph</u>
Good evening! My little one, tonight you have been blessed with sharing in the joy of the nativity of Jesus. You received many graces through this gift from God.

<u>Janie</u>
I am such a bad sinner. I am not worthy to have been given this gift. Can you tell me why?

<u>St. Joseph</u>
My little one, it is not important that you ask why, but that you accept the love and favor that God has shown you. God has blessed you with a responsibility to cultivate the hearts of the family through your prayers and sufferings. God loves you very much, and He entrusted you with a great responsibility. Be thankful and show God your gratitude through your obedience by doing what is asked of you.

Share with all the families that you meet, the importance of love and prayer in their lives. I ask that they trust in my intercession, and I will protect all families who call upon my help. I will draw them closer to God.

Through my intercession there will be peace and love between spouses. I will teach their children the virtues of obedience and purity. Their homes will be homes of peace and joy. I, St. Joseph, will protect all families who call upon my intercession. I will love them and take care of them as I did Most Holy Mary and Jesus.

I am Your Mother Come from Heaven to Love You

Teaching from St. Joseph, December 24, 1993 (Continued)

I wish that all families continue to consecrate their family to the Sacred Heart of Jesus and the Immaculate Heart of Mary and to my intercession.

I, St. Joseph, invite all families to begin a new life, a new walk with God. If my request is heeded, families all over the world will experience God's love like never before. Families will return back to God, and God will forgive all their sinfulness.

I, St. Joseph, speak also to the all the priests. Open your hearts and live in God's love. Many of you suffer from ridicule and persecution, but when these sufferings come your way, you become angry and bitter. Cast all your concerns to me, St. Joseph, that I may present your concerns to your beloved Brother, Jesus.

Beloved priests, feed the flock entrusted to you by God and live in His peace, live in His peace. On this holy night when the Infant Child was born as Savior of the world and Prince of Peace, allow His peace to reign in your hearts and the Church. I, St. Joseph, give you God's blessing and invite all priests to invoke my intercession, and I will help you in your struggles and in your sufferings. Trust in my intercession.

My little one, this is all for tonight. You have been given much tonight, hold it close to your heart in a special way.

I am Your Mother Come from Heaven to Love You

Message from Our Lord, Jesus, December 25, 1993, 10:55 a.m.
Christmas Day

I was sitting at home in my living room and a great heaviness flooded my heart. I was filled with sorrow and grief. I began to cry, and Jesus was with me. He showed me the many hearts that do not know Him. I got up and went to our prayer room to pray.

Janie
Lord, help me. I pray to You for my own selfish and sinful heart. Show me how to love You, Lord.

Jesus
My child, you are sharing in My sorrow for all those souls who reject Me. Their souls are filled with sin and they have not repented. They walk in darkness; they have refused My love and My invitation for them to live in My peace.

I, the Prince of Peace, came for all, young and old. I am the Prince of Peace and Truth, but many have refused to live in My truth. There is much darkness in the world. Evil reigns in the hearts of many. The cup of sinfulness is overflowing because of the refusal to live in My truth and light.

My child, this is the sadness that has filled your heart. For I, your Savior, wanted to share My sorrow with you, for I know that your heart is Mine. I love you. I love you. Pray for all that I have shown you.

I am Your Mother Come from Heaven to Love You

Message from Jesus and Our Mother of Compassion and Love,
December 25, 1993, 3:00 p.m.
Christmas Day

PROCESSION OF THE HOLY SOULS

Jesus
Welcome, My child, and thank you for coming. Prepare to witness the great rejoicing of the Holy Souls as they are taken to Heaven. Write down everything that you see.

Janie
I prayed to the Holy Spirit to prepare my heart. Then I was silent.

I find myself in a place surrounded by great light. I see an opening in the heavens, and great light is pouring down into Purgatory. I see Purgatory as a huge cave, but to the top there is an opening which the light from Heaven is coming through. I see what appears to be a golden street or a path, and to each side of the path I see thousands of angels, big and small, singing hymns and praising God.

Our Lady and Jesus, both with golden crowns on Their heads and arrayed in golden garments, escort thousands of souls to Heaven. I see priests, nuns, bishops, old and young people with Jesus and Mary leading and escorted by thousands of angels in procession, going up into this opening in Heaven. As they enter the opening, Mary is to the left and Jesus to the right. The souls enter this light and disappear in the light.

The singing becomes louder, and the rejoicing increases. The procession continues. It's like a parade of souls marching toward Heaven. All wear beautiful white garments, and as they get closer to Heaven, their garments change and become multi-colored. Then, before my eyes, the garments turn to a yellow gold, and then the souls disappear.

More and more continue in procession, and as they pass, they acknowledge my presence and smile at me and thank me. Many of my relatives are among the multitude who are in procession to Heaven. I am especially happy and thankful for all the many priests and religious that entered Heaven today.

Message from Jesus and Our Mother, December 25, 1993
(Continued)

My two brothers, who died years ago are going to Heaven this very day. I am surrounded by great light and rejoicing, and I am so happy to be seeing all this. To me it is like a movie with a huge picture screen with such living colors.

There are great big angels at the opening path that I think is Purgatory. These angels blow their long golden thin trumpets, and more Holy Souls come out in procession.

When they get to Heaven, the angels on that end blow their trumpets as if to announce them. This procession continues and Jesus and Mary with a multitude of angels escort thousands of souls to Heaven. The great light that surrounds me makes me feel such joy in my heart. I feel as though I myself have died and gone to Heaven.

Jesus and Mary come to where I am, and these are Their words. I say Their words, because I can feel both of Their Hearts speaking to my heart (Their Hearts being one). I cannot explain, but it comes from both of Their Hearts.

Jesus and Mary
Our dear child, you have found favor with God, for He chose you to witness the joyful celebration of this special day, when many souls go to Heaven. You, Our dear child, pray much for the Holy Souls. Your prayers and the prayers of many others have helped to release many souls from Purgatory. Their time of suffering has ended, and now they are rejoicing with God in Heaven.

Our dear child, continue to intercede for all the Holy Souls in Purgatory, and rejoice for what you have been graced to witness. Your own heart will never be the same, for you have experienced a little of God's majesty and power. God loves you very much, for He knows that your only desire is to do His Holy Will; for this you are blessed. Go in God's peace and never forget the power of intercessory prayer. We love you, and Our love is with you everywhere you go.

OUR LADY TOLD ME THAT FROM 12 MIDNIGHT ON THE 24TH OF DECEMBER, UNTIL 12 MIDNIGHT ON THE 25TH OF DECEMBER THOUSANDS OF SOULS GO TO HEAVEN.

I am Your Mother Come from Heaven to Love You

Message from Our Lord Jesus in The Blessed Sacrament
December 25, 1993, 6:00 p.m.

Jesus to me after Confession and hearing my prayer.

Jesus
My child, your prayer has pleased Me. My child, today, I have provided you with everything.

(Jesus meant Confession and all the other experiences that He shared with me).

Come and stay with Me, and you will be able to avoid falling into temptation; for when you fall, I will quickly pick you up and rescue you from the hands of the evil one.

My child, you belong to Me, and if you stay with Me, you will learn to resist temptation, for through Me you will overcome sinning. I will be your strength. Do not worry any more about your relationship with your _____. I will take care of this matter for you. You see how much I love you. Be at peace.

I am Your Mother Come from Heaven to Love You

Message from Jesus, December 26, 1993, 10:20 a.m.
After Holy Mass, Feast of The Holy Family

While I was going to receive Holy Communion, I saw the Holy Family where the priest was giving Communion. St. Joseph and Mary were kneeling and Jesus was giving Communion.

The way that I saw Jesus giving Communion (or the way that each individual would receive Him), as they came up to receive Him, He would embrace each individual. The altar was crowded with angels who were prostrated before Jesus. Later, after Mass, I went before the Blessed Sacrament to give thanks.

Janie
Dear Jesus, I saw You, Most Holy Mary, and St. Joseph. I am so happy.

Jesus
That was a gift for you, so that you understand the importance of the Holy Family in your life. Consecrate your family to the Holy Family every day, and you will have peace in your family. Through consecrating your family to the Holy Family, you will be protected from daily temptation.

My child?

Janie
Yes, my Jesus.

Jesus
Did you notice how much holiness your heart felt as you gazed upon the Holy Family?

Janie
Yes, my Jesus, oh yes!

Jesus
When you consecrate your family to the intercession of the Holy Family, you will live in holiness.

207

I am Your Mother Come from Heaven to Love You

Message from Our Mother of Compassion and Love
December 30, 1993

Dear children, today, I, your heavenly Mother, invite you to continue to pray for peace in your family and peace in the world.

My children, prepare through much strong prayer for the coming of the New Year, for it will be a difficult year with much suffering. I invite you to live my messages like never before and to take refuge in the Sacred Heart of my Son and in my Most Immaculate Heart.

My little ones, you are entering into a time of great tribulation where you will see much suffering and violence. You will see changes in the world and in the Church that will frighten you. The Church will undergo much suffering, and many of my beloved priests will be put to the test. Many will suffer persecution, and many will want to flee from the priesthood because of the great persecution.

I turn to you, my children, and ask you and your family to pray with me for my beloved priests. Together, through prayer these changes and sufferings will be lessened. Pray especially for my beloved Pope, for he will endure much suffering due to the persecution and suffering in the Church. Offer up all your prayers and sacrifices in reparation for the needs of all my beloved priests.

My little ones, I invite you to remain close as a family and to remain loving to one another. Protect your children through your prayers, for Satan is very active in trying to destroy the family. He is luring your children through means of drugs and unhealthy influences. It is important that you as parents demonstrate much love towards your children. Pray together every day your Rosary. Many of you have been neglecting family prayer. You put other activities before prayer.

My children, listen to your heavenly Mother; prayer is important, especially praying the Rosary. Prayer brings you peace. I invite you to consecrate your families to my Immaculate Heart, and I will protect you. I will lead you closer to my Son.

Message from Our Mother December 30, 1993 (Continued)

My children, I invite you to help me in the battle to disarm Satan. Remember, these are your weapons against Satan: prayer, fasting, the Holy Rosary, Adoration, Holy Mass, and receiving frequently the sacrament of Reconciliation. I invite you not to be afraid but to have faith, not to talk about prayer but to pray, not to talk about my messages but live them. If you respond to my request, you will help to usher in the reign of my Immaculate Heart. Through your prayers many will convert. Pray, pray, pray. Thank you for listening to my message.

Message from Our Lord Jesus in the Blessed Sacrament
December 31, 1993

Welcome to My Eucharistic Heart. My Child, tonight, I, Jesus, bless you and your family with My love, joy and My peace. Remain in My love, so that you may be one with Me as I am one with My Father. If you remain in My love, you and your family will be able to live through these troubled times.

This new year marks a difficult year with much suffering throughout the world. Abandon yourself to My love and trust Me. Listen to My words, My child, and you will embrace all the difficulties that lie ahead with a joyful heart. My love will see you through everything. Remain in My love, and you will have joy, peace and strength. I now give you My blessing to share with your family.

I am Your Mother Come from Heaven to Love You

Message from Our Mother of Compassion and Love
January 4, 1994

URGENT MESSAGE

Dear Child,

It is my desire that unceasing prayer and fasting be offered in reparation to end the war in Bosnia. If my children respond to my request, the war will dissolve through your prayers. Trust in the Two Hearts in this effort. Pray and fast unceasingly to end this horrible war that has taken so many innocent victims.

My child, you will not go wrong in this effort, but through your obedience in responding to my request, special blessings will be bestowed upon my children who join you in this effort. Trust your heavenly Mother, trust your heavenly Mother. Share this with my son. (She meant Fr. Henry).

Janie
My beloved Mother, I will share this message with Fr. Henry. I ask that you intercede for me for enlightenment from the Holy Spirit.

Blessed Mother, I will begin to invite others to join me. We will pray around the clock (if it's okay with Fr. Henry). We will offer our Holy Mass, Rosary, Adoration, and fasting. We will sign up for a certain hour to pray. I will ask others to commit to one of these three: Holy Mass, praying the Rosary, or Adoration.

We will pray this way until your request is met to have as many of your children praying around the clock as possible. Do you approve of this plan, my Mother?

Our Lady
Yes, my child, yes. Through this effort, my children will learn to be committed to prayer in their daily needs. My children will learn the importance of prayer and fasting. Thank you, my child, for helping your heavenly Mother.

I am Your Mother Come from Heaven to Love You

Message from Our Mother of Compassion and Love
January 4, 1994

Dear children, today, I invite you and your family to offer all your prayers and sacrifices in reparation for the war in Bosnia. Pray for my children who are victims of this war that has lasted so long.

My little ones, trust in my Immaculate Heart and turn to your heavenly Mother with all your family concerns. In this way I will protect you. Many of you suffer, and in your suffering you forget to pray. You allow your suffering to become a distraction for you.

Remember, my children, that God hears all your prayers. Through your prayers the hearts of those you are praying for begin to change. Trust in God and in my intercession with all your struggles.

My children, you have begun a new year. Let this year be a year full of prayer and peace. You know that this will be a difficult year with much suffering. Do not be afraid, my children, for I am with you each step of the way. I will never abandon you.

Allow your prayers to transform your lives. In this way you will help your heavenly Mother to lead you to purity and holiness. Through my intercession I will deflect all the temptations that Satan will put in your path. Abandon yourselves to the Two Hearts, and you will overcome all fear. I love you all, my children. I am praying with you and for all of your intentions. Thank you for listening to my message.

211

I am Your Mother Come from Heaven to Love You

Teaching from St. Joseph, January 7, 1994, 9:40 p.m.

St. Joseph
Good evening, my little one. I bring you God's peace.

Janie
Oh, good evening, St. Joseph. Thank you, thank you for coming. I missed you.

(He had not come on Friday, New Year's Eve, due to my family's celebration).

St. Joseph
My little one, it is so good to be here with you. I, St. Joseph, look forward to this time that we spend together. Is there anything in particular on which you wish me to give you guidance?

Janie
Yes, my beloved St. Joseph. Lately, I've been having problems with being truly committed to my prayer time. I am being distracted through much social injustice that occurs in my work place.

Please help me and teach me how to remain detached from everything which is not from the Lord. I do not want to develop a judgmental attitude towards others. I am unhappy about these distractions. Please give me divine guidance.

St. Joseph
My little one, you must abandon yourself completely to God, allowing yourself to become deaf and blind to the things of the world, so that you may become completely absorbed by the presence of God in your life.

Janie
How do I become deaf and blind to the world? I don't understand.

St. Joseph
My little one, in order to do this, you have to put God first in your life. You must hunger only for purity and holiness of heart. You have to be totally detached from everything in your life which distracts you from doing the Will of God.

Teaching from St. Joseph, January 7, 1994 (Continued)

Give every second of the day to serving God in everything you do. You must resist all temptations around you and all distractions. Love everyone around you, for each individual is God's creation.

No matter what others say or do, do not imitate their attitudes, but relate to them with a loving attitude and in a spiritual manner. Allow everyone to see the Christ in you by your attitude. Avoid gossip and all things that do not come from God. Imitate the life of Jesus and be the reflection of Most Holy Mary. Have a joyful attitude and do not be self seeking, but seek God in everything. You must never allow yourself to separate from God, but pray, so that through your prayer you may be one with God.

Listen to my words and guidance. Live my instructions and teachings. Only in this way will you be deaf to the things of the world and hear the things that are from God. My teachings and guidance will help you to close your eyes to the things of he world and open your eyes to the things that are of God. My little one, this is the path that will lead you to sanctity and purity.

<u>Janie</u>
Beloved St. Joseph, you are so good and kind. I thank God for you. I am so excited and happy for the guidance that you have given me tonight. Please pray for all my family and friends. Please intercede for the war in Bosnia. I love you most humble St. Joseph. Thank you.

<u>St. Joseph</u>
Good night, my little one. I will intercede for all your intentions. Remain and live in God's true peace.

I am Your Mother Come from Heaven to Love You

Message from Our Mother of Compassion and Love
January 10, 1994

Dear children, today, I invite you to trust in my intercession. Take refuge in my Most Immaculate Heart, and I will lead you to holiness and purity of heart.

My little ones, continue to pray as a family and live my messages. Pray for my children that live in darkness, whose hearts are closed to my Son, Jesus.

My children, pray to the Holy Spirit for enlightenment in all your decisions in your daily lives. He will help you to live God's Holy Will.

My children, decide for conversion, for my time with you is short. Open your hearts and abandon your lives to the Two Hearts. Do not be afraid of the world that continues to live in sin. Convert, convert, before it is too late!

Pray for my beloved Pope, and all my beloved priests. Pray and offer your sufferings for my Church. Pray, my children, pray, so that God will help my Church to remain united to my Son during the great tribulation. Thank you for listening to my message.

Message from Our Mother of Compassion and Love
San Antonio, Texas, January 15, 1994

Dear children, today, I greet each one with my motherly love. Know, my children, that I, your heavenly Mother, brought you all here to bless you. As you pray together, I will be praying with you, my children. You have brought much joy to my Immaculate Heart.

My children, many of you are sad and suffering. You have come looking for answers to your prayers. Many of you have physical pains, and you are hurting. Abandon everything to my Immaculate Heart, and I will help you and bless you. Have no worry, for you, my children, are all under my shadow and protection.

I am Your Mother Come from Heaven to Love You

Message from Our Mother of Compassion and Love
January 20, 1994, 7:15 a.m.

Dear children, today, I invite all families to continue to pray together and to live in my Son's love.

Today, I wish to thank you for all your efforts to remain strong in prayer during hard times.

My children, I invite you to be living witnesses of my messages. I say this, my children, because so many of you are eager to read my messages, but you do not put them into practice.

My children, God's mercy is being demonstrated to each one of you by allowing me to remain with you for so long. Today, I ask you, my children, what more can I do for you? I have been teaching you the importance of prayer, fasting, and loving one another. I have been teaching you that through prayer and fasting, conversion will come easy for those who desire to convert. Through all my time with you I have invited you to be reconciled back to God and be converted.

My children, all it takes to be my children is to say "yes" to me and to live my messages. Know, my children, that the most recent earthquake and its severity was lessened through all your prayers and sacrifices. Through your prayers many lives were saved, for this I extend my gratitude to all. Continue to pray and know that God hears all your prayers. Thank you for listening to my message.

I am Your Mother Come from Heaven to Love You

Teaching from St. Joseph, January 21, 1994
Austin, Texas

My Beloved Young People,

I, St. Joseph, bring you God's love and peace. I greet each one of you. Know, my young ones, that you are all special to God. He has great blessings for you.

This evening, I, St. Joseph, ask you to open your hearts to God and to place your complete trust in Him. He knows everything about you. He knows all your sufferings. There aren't any secrets in your hearts that God does not know. You cannot conceal anything from Him Who created you with all His love and tenderness.

My beloved ones, I, St. Joseph, know of the questions in your hearts. Some of you are struggling with your faith. Tonight, I, St. Joseph, will help you with the questions that you ponder in your hearts.

Listen, my young ones, and listen with your hearts. Ask the Holy Spirit to enlighten your hearts as I speak to you. You question the mercy of God, and you wonder why He allows His children to suffer.

Know that God's heart is full of love and mercy for all His children. He does not want His children to suffer. Suffering is the result of disobedience and many other natural causes. God invites all His children to be reconciled to His love and mercy and to be converted.

It is important that in your suffering, you examine your heart to understand the reason for your suffering. Much suffering in the world today is due to lack of love and charity. Those who have been blessed with wealth, choose not to share their blessings with the less fortunate. Those individuals who are loving and charitable, they are the ones that make the world a better place to live, for their hearts are set on doing the Will of God through helping others.

My little ones, you wonder why certain spouses have children and others do not. God alone knows the reason. He wants you to trust Him, for He knows what is best for you. I want you to know that, whether you have children or not, God considers you a family. As a family you are called to love one another, including your siblings who at times make it difficult for you to love them.

216

Teaching from St. Joseph, January 21, 1994 (Continued)

You wonder about the Rosary and whether it helps you when you pray as a family. Know that praying the family Rosary helps you to love one another and to forgive one another. The family that prays the Rosary receives many blessings and graces. They grow together and they grow closer to God. Pray your Rosary every day.

My little ones, you ask if music is bad for you. You want to know what kind of music to listen to. Know that music can be beautiful; the angels are forever singing praises to God. You must pray to be selective about the music that you listen to. Avoid all music which has profanity, music in which the words identify more with death than living. You must avoid all music that makes you feel sad. Listen to music that teaches you about God and His love. Do not listen to music that will distract you from God. Pray to the Holy Spirit. He will enlighten you.

There are some of you who are concerned about your careers. You wonder what God is calling you to. Do not worry, but pray and God will manifest His plan for you. Trust Him.

To you who are called to be teachers, use the gift wisely. Teach your students, especially children and adolescents about God and His Commandments. You must pray every day, so that God will enlighten you and help you to be a loving teacher. Be gentle in your teaching and be Christ-like. Teach with love and gentleness in your hearts. Pray for the families of those you teach and love them like God loves you.

My little ones, some of you are worried about the discipline you receive from your parents, and whether they are doing what is right for you. Pray for your parents and be obedient to them, and God will reward you.

To those of you who are concerned about choosing the right spouse, again, I say, trust God with everything, and He will answer your prayers.

You wonder if it is important to go to church. My little ones, when you go to church you are honoring one of God's Ten Commandments. He wants you to go to church, so that you may draw closer to Him.

Teaching from St. Joseph, January 21, 1994 (Continued)

Some of you have asked if it was hard for me to be with Jesus and Most Holy Mary. My little ones, it was an honor and blessing for me to be chosen by God for such a wonderful mission. Throughout my time on earth, I trusted God completely with my heart and soul. You must do the same!

My little ones, you ask what is Heaven like and what do the saints do in Heaven. In Heaven, there is eternal love and joy. No words are necessary. There is no worry, no sadness, no needs, only joy. Once you are in Heaven, you have no needs, for you are united with God the Father. In Heaven there is perpetual bliss.

Heaven should be your only goal! You obtain this goal through prayer, going to church, reading Holy Scripture. You must love those around you and respect your parents. Doing God's Will on earth will help you in your faith journey and in your path to Heaven.

My little ones, pray and trust God. Begin your day with prayer and end your day with prayer. Do not forget how much God loves you. His love will protect you from all the violence, the drugs, the killings, fornication, unhealthy music and relationships. Yes, my little ones, God will protect you if you trust Him and if you pray. He will provide you with everything: good parents, teachers, and spiritual directors.

Love one another and believe in God. Satan is trying to destroy you, but through your prayers you can overcome all his temptations. I tell you again, do not leave your homes without praying. Be obedient to your parents and pray for them. Be examples to your friends and help them by praying for them. Love them and forgive them when they hurt you.

My little ones, now is the time for love. Now is the time to respond to God's love and mercy. Abandon yourselves to the Sacred Heart of Jesus and the Immaculate Heart of Mary.

My beloved ones, live my guidance and trust in my intercession. I, St. Joseph, will help you. Do not be afraid. Allow God's love to live in your hearts. I give you God's blessings. Peace to all, peace to all.

I am Your Mother Come from Heaven to Love You

Message from Our Mother of Compassion and Love
January 25, 1994, 8:10 a.m.

Dear children, today, I invite you to abandon yourselves to my Son's love and mercy. Do not procrastinate, my children, but enter into my Son's love and mercy and be converted!

My children, remember, prayer is your strength, so pray, pray, pray! Do not be sad and do not quarrel with one another, but love one another. Satan is active in causing so many families to quarrel. His one goal is to separate you from God and to take His peace from you. Do not give into Satan's temptations, but pray together as a family. I say again, love one another and live in God's peace, for where there is God's love and peace, Satan has no power.

My children, listen to your heavenly Mother and take refuge in the Two Hearts; in this way no evil will harm you. Continue to pray and make reparation for the war in Bosnia. Do not abandon this effort, but be committed! Together, we can bring an end to this horrible war. Thank you for listening to my message.

I am Your Mother Come from Heaven to Love You

Teaching from St. Joseph, January 28, 1994

St. Joseph
Good evening, my little one.

Janie
Good evening, St. Joseph, and thank you for coming. Thanks be to God for being so good to me.

St. Joseph
My little one, you had a hard time today, but you remained faithful to praying throughout your crisis.

Janie
Yes, my beloved St. Joseph, today was hard for me, and I thank you for helping me to continue to be loving through it all.

(Today, we had numerous problems. I didn't get much sleep last night. I prayed much and woke up very tired).

St. Joseph
My little one, you have been suffering interiorly and silently. Tell me, so that I may be able to help you in your suffering.

Janie
Beloved St. Joseph, I am getting nervous about the celebration of my fifth anniversary with my Blessed Mother. I have a sadness in my heart, for I have a knowing in my heart that she won't be visiting me much longer. I also feel this way about your visitations to me. It saddens my heart, for I never had anything so beautiful happen to me. Through these experiences, I feel that I have drawn closer to God. This makes me happy, but sad at the same time. I can't describe exactly how I feel.

My beloved St. Joseph, I don't mean to say that I am not grateful to God for these blessings. I am having mixed feelings. On the other hand, I am very happy about the celebration on February 15th.

Teaching from St. Joseph, January 28, 1994 Continued)

<u>St. Joseph</u>
My little one, rejoice and show God your gratitude by offering your suffering in reparation for those many souls who walk in darkness. God knows your heart and your sadness. Know, my little one, that this celebration will be a heavenly blessing to all who come. God will demonstrate His love and mercy on this day. Many will experience a glimpse of Heaven in their souls, others will receive answers to their prayers.

God will bestow extraordinary graces to those who come with open hearts. All are invited to show their gratitude by embracing their heavenly Mother on this day.

Most Holy Mary will embrace all her children who come from near and far. Her beloved priests will receive special graces and blessings to help them in their faith journey. Their heavenly Mother will take all her priests under her motherly mantle, and she will hold them tenderly to her Immaculate Heart for being obedient in honoring her on this day in a special way.

All who come will be under the mantle of their heavenly Mother. She will receive all her children. She will bless them and love them as a mother loves her children.

Yes, my little one, this will truly be a special day for your church. Your neighborhood will receive blessings from Heaven. So I, St. Joseph, ask you, my little one, not to be sad, but rejoice and continue preparing through your prayer for this joyous occasion. You will not regret it!

I, St. Joseph, ask you to look to Most Holy Mary for motherly guidance. Model after her, for she is the reflection of her Son, Jesus, Who is your Savior and Lord. Look to your heavenly Mother, for she is the Queen of Heaven. She is the gate that leads you to her Son. She is your Mother who loves you as her little child. Love your Mother, and take refuge in her Immaculate Heart and have no worry. When the time comes for her to stop coming to you, she will not abandon you. Her Spouse, the Holy Spirit, will continue to enlighten you to live God's Most Holy Will. Abandon all worries and sadness and embrace your heavenly Mother who is embracing you. Again, I, St. Joseph, tell you that great blessings will be given to all who come to honor their heavenly Mother. Good night.

I am Your Mother Come from Heaven to Love You

Message from Our Lord Jesus in the Blessed Sacrament
January 29, 1994

Welcome to My Eucharistic Heart. Come, My child, spend a few moments with your Jesus of Love and Mercy. Know that you console My Eucharistic Heart when you come to visit Me.

Tell your Savior everything that is bothering you. Trust Me, and I will take away everything that distracts you from loving Me. I am a jealous Savior. I want all your love and all your trust. I want your complete attention.

Allow Me to help you to become a slave of love, so that you may only have one desire: to love everyone and to have a loving and merciful heart like your beloved Savior.

Come, My child, come to your Jesus of Love and Mercy. Come, be a slave of love and remain united to My love for all eternity.

Message from Our Mother of Compassion and Love
January 31, 1994, 8:15 a.m.

Dear children, today, I invite you to continue to decide for conversion as a family. Pray your family Rosary every day! Remember, the Rosary is your weapon, and through praying the Rosary, you draw closer to God day by day.

My children, again, I ask you to trust in my motherly intercession. In this way I will be able to help you and to lead you closer to my Son.

Remember, my children, that you must pray. If you do not pray, I cannot help you. Satan is busy trying to destroy you as a family. He has already separated many families, because they do not pray. I invite you, as a family, to pray for other families, so that through your prayers they may decide for conversion. Please my children, do everything I invite you to do, and do not delay in your decision to live my messages!

I am Your Mother Come from Heaven to Love You

Message from January 31, 1994 (Continued)

My children, pray for my beloved Pope and for all my priests, that they too will help their heavenly Mother to lead others to my Son through their prayers and efforts.

I invite you, dear children, to open your hearts to the love and mercy of my Son, Jesus. Spend time with Him in prayer. Remember, He knows your hearts. Come to Him, little children, and be converted. Pray, children, pray, for through prayer you discover God's love. Thank you for listening to my message.

Teaching from St. Joseph, February 4, 1994, 5:45 p.m.

Janie
St. Joseph, thank you for coming. Thank you for coming. I need your help tonight. I don't know why I feel the way that I do, but I am so thankful that you are here.

St. Joseph
Good evening, my little one. I, St. Joseph, am here to help you. Tell me what is bothering you.

Janie
Oh St. Joseph, there is so much that I want you to help me with. You know, St. Joseph, that I only want to do God's Holy Will, but sometimes this is so hard. Tell me beloved St. Joseph, how can I serve God?

I want to be a loving and good wife, and a loving and good mother. This is hard for me at times. I love my family with all my heart, but sometimes I feel that they don't understand my role as a mother and wife. At times I make decisions that are not very popular, and my family gets upset with me. This hurts me very much. Tell me what to do.

St. Joseph
My little one, you are being too hard on yourself. Your family loves you and respects you even when you have to make decisions which are against their desires.

I am Your Mother Come from Heaven to Love You

Teaching from St. Joseph, February 4, 1994 (Continued)

All families have disagreements from time to time. That is why it is important that a family has love and prayer as its foundation. In this way, when they disagree, they are able to be reconciled to one another through their love and through the many blessings and graces that come through prayer.

The blessings and graces that are received through prayer are like merits that can be applied in times of difficulties and sufferings in the family. The power of prayer is beyond human understanding. God sees all good deeds, and He rewards all His children for all their good efforts.

My little one, do not dwell on family disagreements, but waste no time and be reconciled by forgiving one another. A family is a blessing from God, but a loving and prayerful family is truly filled with God's Holy Spirit. They are illuminated by the flame of God's love. A loving and prayerful family will be able to overcome all trials and tribulations, because God's favor rests on them.

My little one, you have been blessed with a loving and prayerful family, and God's favor rests on your family. Rejoice, then, and demonstrate your gratitude by allowing God's Spirit to illuminate others through you.

My little one, your family will be your strength in times of difficulty, as you are their strength. Continue to pray together as a family and trust God in every situation.

Janie
Oh, beloved St. Joseph, I knew that you would help me to see my situation through the eyes of my soul. Now I understand how our prayers and our love help us as a family. I love you Most Holy St. Joseph, I love you. Thank you from the bottom of my heart and soul. I will live your teachings, for your teachings come from God.

St. Joseph
My little one, you are dear to my heart. Remain obedient to my teachings and you will be able to follow the path that leads to purity and holiness.

Good evening, my little one. You are dear to my heart.

I am Your Mother Come from Heaven to Love You

Message from Our Mother of Compassion and Love
February 10, 1994, 9:15 a.m.

Dear children, today, I invite you to prepare your hearts through prayer and fasting to receive all the graces and blessings that God wishes to bestow upon you and your family.

My children, I know that many of you are experiencing much suffering in your family. Many of you have allowed your suffering to become a distraction for you, and you choose not to pray. Remember, my children, that through prayer you discover God, and prayer brings you God's peace.

My little children, abandon yourselves to the Two United Hearts with filial trust. Do not allow your suffering to cause you to fear. Remember, that with God all things are possible. Trust in your prayers and remain true to serving God with joy in your hearts.

Continue praying your family Rosary and cling to God's love and mercy in your suffering. He will inflame your hearts with His Holy Spirit to help you and guide you in everything. Peace, my children, peace. Live my messages and be converted! Thank you for listening to my message.

I am Your Mother Come from Heaven to Love You

Message from Jesus in the Blessed Sacrament
February 10, 1994, 1:30 p.m.

MESSAGE REGARDING THE CELEBRATION HONORING
OUR LADY ON FEBRUARY 15TH

My Child,

Be at peace, for it is I, Who am working through you. You must remain in a spirit of prayer to receive all the graces and blessings that My Father wants to give to you on that day. Ask Me for anything, for anything you ask of My Father in My Name, He will do.

There will be one angel from each choir with the child that represents that choir, and the virtue of that choir will remain in the heart of that child forever.

Heaven will open up and the light of Heaven will shine this day on the community of St. Julia and on everyone who comes. All who come will carry this light. All who come are responding to My personal invitation.

My Father is pleased with your work, and you will not regret anything that you are doing. It is a joy to participate in a heavenly task such as this one.

My Mother is preparing her spiritual ark in many cities and towns where she is not yet known, so that when the time comes that she will no longer be with you, her Spouse, the Holy Spirit will be with you in such a powerful way, such a powerful way!

In this way, it is necessary that when My Mother's time is up, she will usher in the Holy Spirit to every heart that has been open to her messages. As the stars illuminate the night, you will be like stars that illuminate the day - like light upon light, because God's divine light has been inflamed in your hearts by the power of the Holy Spirit.

Each person who is coming to this sacred gathering has a personal mission that they have been invested with. Many who come for the first time will discover the calling of God in a special way, and they are going to go out and fulfill their roles.

Message from Jesus, February 10, 1994 (Continued)

Out of this sacred gathering will result rivers of living water. In this way, long after you go to your homeland, which is Heaven, you will leave behind rivers of living water, which will be hearts illuminated with the Holy Spirit. I solemnly tell you that all that I am giving you will come to pass. I give you My word.

I am Your Mother Come from Heaven to Love You

Teaching from St. Joseph, February 11, 1994

THERE WILL BE CONVERSION IN MANY HEARTS

Good evening, my little one. I, St. Joseph, thank you for all your efforts and your suffering. Know that God is pleased with all your efforts and sacrifices.

Janie
Good evening, St. Joseph. Thank you for waiting so patiently for me, for I've had so much work to finish. I know it's late, but my husband wanted me to finish cleaning up, so I thought I'd better do that, so that he wouldn't be upset with me.

St. Joseph, God is so good to me by allowing you to come and visit me, yet I don't seem to be grateful. I say this because this week has been so hard for me. There is so much suffering in my family and in my work place.

I have been angry with others around me, and I haven't trusted God in my struggles. Please, beloved St. Joseph, intercede for me, so that God will forgive me for allowing my suffering to be a distraction for me.

St. Joseph
My dear little one, God has forgiven you for everything. He knows your capabilities, and He won't test you beyond your strength. My little one, know that all your own suffering and the suffering in your family is helping you to draw closer together as a family. You see, my little one, God has chosen you and your family to be an example to other families.

Through all your trials and tribulations, you are growing in wisdom as a family. You are able to love and accept one another, even though you may disagree, your love for one another is stronger than any disruption that Satan puts in your path. As a family, God allows you to be tested, for He knows that He is the center of your lives. He is pleased with you and your family. Have no fear and continue to pray together.

I am Your Mother Come from Heaven to Love You

Teaching from St. Joseph, February 11, 1994 (Continued)

<u>Janie</u>
Oh, St. Joseph, your words bring so much comfort to my heart. Your words give me strength. I promise that I will continue to love and help my family instead of getting upset.

<u>St. Joseph</u>
My little one, know that your reward is great in Heaven. Embrace all your suffering with joy in your heart. All your suffering helps to bring others closer to God, for you, my little one, are God's chosen victim soul.

Your suffering has the fragrance of purity and holiness, for you suffer without complaining and without asking God to take your suffering away. You accept your suffering, and you accept it all without reservation.

My little one, do not allow Satan to fill your heart with his lies, but remain strong and cling to God's love in all your suffering. As a family, pray to the Holy Spirit. Consecrate your day to the Holy Spirit. Pray with Him all day. The Holy Spirit will enlighten your hearts with the wisdom that comes from the very heart of the Eternal Father.

Trust the Holy Spirit as a family. He is the One Who will teach you and guide you in your daily walk. Prepare your hearts, for on your anniversary you and your family will receive an abundance of special graces and blessings to help you as a family.

All who come will experience a glimpse of the glory and joy of Heaven. There will be conversion in many hearts. Many prayers will be answered. Rejoice in this day, for the Heavens will rejoice with you.

My little one, this will be a very special day for those who come. All who come will be a blessing to others, and out of their hearts will be born rivers of living water. The Holy Spirit will inflame their hearts with His eternal fire and love.

Embrace this day with love in your hearts. Most Holy Mary will embrace all her children, all her children. I, St. Joseph, invite all to embrace their heavenly Mother who loves them with heavenly love.

I am Your Mother Come from Heaven to Love You

Teaching from St. Joseph, February 11, 1994 (Continued)

Now, my little one, share all that I, St. Joseph, tell you. It is late.
Receive God's blessings. Sleep in His love. Good night, my little
one. You are so dear to my heart.

Janie
Oh, St. Joseph, you are also dear to my heart. I'll do just as you say.
Good night.

Message from Our Mother of Compassion and Love
February 13, 1994, 8:55 p.m.

My Dear children, I have come to embrace each one of you and to
thank you for all of your work.

My little ones, you are suffering, and you are tired. If you only knew
how much God loves you! If you only knew how much I need your
prayers and even your sufferings.

My children, know that I am here with each one of you. Have no fear
or worry. Know that you are all very special to me, and I hold you all
close to my motherly bosom. Love one another and be patient with
one another, for your rewards are great in Heaven. I love you, my little
ones. Take refuge in my Most Immaculate Heart and be at peace, be
at peace.

I am Your Mother Come from Heaven to Love You

Message from Our Mother of Compassion and Love
February 15, 1994, 8:30 a.m.

FIFTH ANNIVERSARY OF OUR LADY'S VISITATIONS TO JANIE

Dear children, today, I, your heavenly Mother, embrace each one of you. Know that I have brought you here to bless you.

My children, today is a day of great rejoicing, therefore, have no other distractions, but open your hearts to my Immaculate Heart.

Little children, you are all so dear to me. You will never understand the love that I have for you. I ask that you trust in my motherly intercession and abandon yourselves to my Immaculate Heart with filial trust.

My little children, today is a very special day for you and for me. Let us together, give thanks to God for allowing me to remain with you for such a long time.

For a while now, I have been teaching you how to love, how to forgive and how to pray as a family. You have pleased your heavenly Mother through your obedience in living my motherly teaching and messages. You have consoled my Immaculate Heart. You have brought joy to my Heart.

Today, my children, I want to bring God's joy to your hearts. Tell your heavenly Mother what you need. What is bothering you? How can I help you? I am here my children, God has sent me to help you to live by His Commandments.

Come, my children, enter into my Immaculate Heart, which is the gate that will lead you to the Sacred Heart of my Son, Jesus. Trust in the Two Hearts which are one with the Father, and have no fear or worry.* I am here, I am here to protect you.

To my beloved priests, how can I thank you, my beloved sons? Your being here demonstrates your love for your heavenly Mother. Come, my beloved sons, come and allow your heavenly Mother to embrace you with deep gratitude.

Message from Our Mother February 15, 1994 (Continued)

Thank you for feeding the flock entrusted to your care. Your hard work is blessed by God, and He is pleased with you. Know, my beloved sons, that I am with you in everything. Love one another, love one another!

Live my messages and be converted! Today I bless you all. Bring all your worries and anxieties to your heavenly Mother who loves you. Rejoice, rejoice, rejoice! Thank you for listening to my message.

I am Your Mother Come from Heaven to Love You

Message from Jesus in the Blessed Sacrament
February 16, 1994, 3:30 p.m.

Jesus
My dear child, welcome to My Eucharistic Heart. Thank you for coming to spend time with Me, your Jesus Who loves you.

My child, today is a new beginning for you. I, your Jesus, your Eucharistic Savior, invite you to journey with Me for a period of forty days. During this time, I will teach you on virtues that will help you in your own faith journey. Do you accept My invitation, My child?

Janie
Yes, my Lord, I accept your invitation with a joyful heart. Tell me what You would have me do.

Jesus
My child, I have much to ask of you, and you have responded with a total yes. Know how much you please and console My Eucharistic Heart. During the next forty days, you will journey with Me, and I shall take you through a path that few have chosen to travel. It is a hard path with much suffering, so prepare will with strong prayer and fasting.

I shall begin to teach you on virtues that will help you when you are sent out to harvest the hearts of the family. All who hear your words will know that I sent you.

Janie
Even priests, my Lord?

Jesus
Especially My beloved brother priests, for the words that come forth from your mouth will be My words. I, your Eucharistic Jesus, will invest you with wisdom and knowledge that comes from My Father's throne of glory!

Janie
Why are You doing this? Why are You giving me this wisdom and knowledge?

Jesus
My child, you are My humble servant and you have responded with a total yes to My request. You will need the virtues I invest you with, for you will be sent among rebellious and unbelieving people. Hard of face and obstinate of heart are they whom I will send you to. These whom you speak to have resisted the invitation to repent and to turn away from their sins.

Know that many will contradict you and reject you, especially those who call themselves your friends. Fear neither them nor their words, nor be dismayed at their looks for their hearts are without My light and truth.

My child, I, your Jesus, will prepare you for the responsibilities that have been entrusted to you by My Father in Heaven. Do not be concerned with what I am telling you now, but trust Me and later on you will understand. Return to your home now, My child. Go with My love and blessing.

Janie
Thank You, Jesus. I promise I won't allow myself to be concerned with anything.

I am Your Mother Come from Heaven to Love You

Message from Jesus in the Blessed Sacrament
February 17, 1994, 3:30 p.m.

My Dear Child,

Welcome to My Eucharistic Heart. Thank you for your obedience in coming to be with Me and allowing nothing to distract you from coming.

Today, My child, I will speak to you on the virtue of obedience. This virtue will help you to carry out everything that I ask of you. This virtue will help you in all aspects of your life.

My child, obedience is a first class virtue. Obedience leads to sanctity. Through the virtue of obedience you are able to do anything that I ask of you. Obedience is something that I, your Jesus, find most acceptable.

My child, you cannot offer your beloved Savior a more perfect sacrifice than your humble and obedient heart that is ready to do everything that I ask you to do.

My child, open your heart and submit to Me and always be obedient to Me. No matter where you may be, when obedience calls, submit to it as if I, your Jesus, am bodily present at your work, at home, or where ever you are.

Deny your very self and be obedient to Me by being obedient to your husband, to the needs of your family, your pastor, your spiritual director, your supervisors, and friends who need your assistance. By doing this you will please your loving Savior.

My child, do not resist, but yield to My command to embrace the virtue of obedience. Love this virtue with all your heart and soul. Never neglect it as long as you live. Be obedient to others for My sake. Do it without being upset or arguing about it. Remember, you are being obedient to Me in all things, in being obedient to others.

Pray for the grace to leave yourself for My sake by denying your own will. Despise your own wisdom and submit yourself to My command. Rely on Me by relying on your husband, your confessor, pastor, or spiritual director for assistance. Do nothing without spiritual advice from those I put in your path.

235

Message from Jesus February 17, 1994 (Continued)

My child, love in simplicity and poverty of spirit. Renounce your very own self and all your knowledge and rely on your beloved Savior in everything.

My child, much is being asked of you as a child of My Father; that is why you must learn about the virtue of obedience. You will be able to be obedient by denying your very self. Abandon your own will and judgment, and embrace My Will - the virtue of obedience.

I love you, My child, and I am calling you to be My reflection in all things by being obedient to all My commands. Every day, abandon yourself to My Father's Holy Will and pick up your cross and follow Me. Learn to die to yourself, that I may be born in you. Love Me and submit to being a slave to the virtue of obedience, and you will bring many souls to Me, your Jesus of Love and Mercy. As I was obedient to My Father, you too, are called to be an obedient servant. Love obedience, love obedience.

I am Your Mother Come from Heaven to Love You

Teaching from St. Joseph, February 18, 1994

<u>St. Joseph</u>
Good evening, my little one. I bring you God's peace. Thank you for preparing your heart through prayer and fasting.

My little one, what can I do to help you? Tonight you are suffering and you are feeling weak.

<u>Janie</u>
Yes, my beloved St. Joseph, I am suffering, but it is for my Savior's sake. I don't mind, really, I don't mind.

<u>St. Joseph</u>
My child, you have a generous and loving heart. God will bless all your efforts. Do you have any special need, my little one?

<u>Janie</u>
Yes, but it's hard for me to write down anything, for all my body hurts. Please pray for me for the grace to be able to write what you tell me.

St. Joseph, I have been a bit concerned with the role of the wife. You have said that the wife's place is in the home. What about the parents who are in need of extra income and what about the single parents? They have need to work, so that they can support and provide for their family.

<u>St. Joseph</u>
My little one, I know that many families have much financial need, and that they must go out and work. I, St. Joseph, invite these families to put God first in their lives and to trust God with everything.

It is important that spouses pray together for discernment before the wife goes out into the work force. A wife must pray for enlightenment from the Holy Spirit, so that she may find the job that is appropriate for the schedule of her family.

Children should never be left alone to take care of one another. An adult must be over the supervision of the children to protect them from any harm. Spouses must pray for God to help them to find caretakers that believe in God. Children must not be left to the care of just anyone; this could only serve to create more problems in the family.

237

I am Your Mother Come from Heaven to Love You

Teaching from St. Joseph, February 18, 1994 (Continued)

Wives must seek jobs that will not take them away from home all the time. Parents must pray, so that they can begin to understand the importance of being with their children as much as possible. Time is precious, and time slips away quickly. Children grow and develop in maturity. They need their parents to be around, so that they feel secure and loved.

When spouses spend much time working, their children learn to depend on other available resources. This is the time that the young turn to drugs, alcohol, sex, stealing and many other temptations that the evil one puts in their path.

Spouses must pray to the Holy Spirit to help them to be prudent in all their decisions concerning the family. They should agree to allowing the wife to work, only if it is truly necessary. This applies to the single parents. They must adjust their schedules to spend as much time with their children as possible.

Spouses must not be focused more on being wealthy, than providing for the spiritual needs of their children. Their children are gifts from Heaven. Children should have good loving memories when they think of their parents. Spouses should provide a loving and prayerful environment for their children.

Spouses must seek the Will of God for their family, so that God may bless their efforts and provide for their well-being. If spouses trust God in their prayer, they will make the right decisions concerning their families needs.

Now, my little one, I, St. Joseph, see that you are suffering. This is all for tonight. I call the blessings of God upon you and your family.

Janie
Thank you, St. Joseph. Pray for me, that I may drink from the cup of my suffering and drink it all.

I am Your Mother Come from Heaven to Love You

Message from Jesus in the Blessed Sacrament
February 18, 1994, 8:20 p.m.

My Beloved Child,

I, your Eucharistic Savior, extend My thanks to you for being here with Me. Open your heart to Me, your Jesus, for I have many blessings which I wish to give to you.

Tonight, I ask you to love your Eucharistic Savior with all your heart. Give Me all your love and hold nothing back. Embrace Me and tell Me what you need to help you to draw closer to My Eucharistic Heart. Tell your Savior all your worries and trust Me to help you.

I shall listen to all your needs, and I shall bless all your efforts. Open your heart to Me, for this is your time to love and embrace Me with all your sufferings and difficulties.

You are sad, because others do not understand My True Presence, and they leave me without ever noticing Me and My Presence among them. Do not be distracted with this, for I want your total attention. I shall hear your prayers for My children who do not yet recognize My True Presence. To pray for them is all I ask of you. Leave them to Me and continue giving Me all your love and attention.

My child, offer all your suffering for My sake and trust Me. I will heal all your woundedness and your broken heart. Abandon yourself to My Eucharistic Heart and surrender all to Me. Allow Me to strip you from all that you've gained and received in the world.

Come to Me in the nakedness of your innocence and allow Me to clothe you with the garment of humility and purity. Allow Me to strip you of everything that the world has offered you. Come to Me and take refuge in My Eucharistic Heart. Love Me with all your heart and with every breath that you take. Trust Me and love Me. Allow nothing to take you away from My love, nothing.

Janie
My Eucharistic Savior, I surrender everything to You, everything. All I have I give You, I hold nothing back. I belong to You.

239

I am Your Mother Come from Heaven to Love You

Message from Our Mother of Compassion and Love
February 21, 1994

Dear children, today, I your heavenly Mother wish to thank each one of you for all your endless hours of hard work. Through your hard efforts and through your generous hearts, many of my children were received with much love.

My children, know that through your obedience to work together to honor your heavenly Mother of Compassion and Love, many of my children who came from all over received an abundance of graces and blessings.

I wish to thank all my children who responded to my Son's invitation to come and embrace their heavenly Mother. God has blessed them, God has blessed them!

To my beloved priests, I, your heavenly Mother embrace each one of you. Many of you, my beloved sons, came, even though you were tired and had busy schedules. Many of you are suffering from persecution and rejection. Do not be distracted with your crosses of suffering and persecution and rejection, but embrace your crosses with joy in your hearts.

Remember, you are all under my motherly mantle and protection. Again, I say, embrace all your crosses for the sake of my Son, Who loves you with deep love. Thank you, my sons, for embracing your Mother and for helping to lead my children closer to God. Thank you all.

My children, continue being loving and compassionate and pray, pray, pray! I love you all, I love you all. Take refuge in my Immaculate Heart and I will lead you to the heart of my Son. Thank you for listening to my message.

I am Your Mother Come from Heaven to Love You

Message from Jesus in the Blessed Sacrament
February 22, 1994, 11:50 a.m.

Dear Child,

You have pleased Me by recognizing your uncharitable attitude. Be loving always, no matter how much others hurt you. Be My reflection in all situations. Trust Me with all your difficulties. Never doubt that I am with you, especially when you feel alone and rejected, for that's when I am My strongest in you. I love you, My child.

Message from Jesus in the Blessed Sacrament
February 23, 1994, 8:10 p.m.

Jesus
My dear child, welcome to My Eucharistic Heart. Come, My child, and enter into My Eucharistic Heart. Allow your beloved Savior to console your aching and sad heart.

Janie
My beloved Lord, I need Your love so much. I wish I could always be by Your side like this in this present moment.

Jesus
What is it, My child? Although I know your heart, tell your Savior your needs. What can I do for you? This time is ours. Speak freely My child, hold nothing back.

Janie
Oh Jesus, sometimes I wish I could be in Heaven with You and Our Lady. I guess I'm feeling sorry for myself. I just need Your love.

Please Jesus, help me. I am sad, because it's so hard for me to spend time with You like I want. My schedule is so busy with my family and my job.

Sometimes, I wish I could go away with You. Help me to be prudent in managing my time well. Help me to bring my family closer to Your loving and Eucharistic Heart. Help us as a family. At times, it is hard to get the family in the spirit of prayer. Tell me what to do.

241

Message from Jesus February 23, 1994 (Continued)

Jesus

My child, share with your family how much I love them. Tell them that the only way to come to know My Eucharistic Heart is through prayer. Through prayer they come to know Me. Prayer helps them to begin a beautiful relationship with Me. As they pray more, their hearts begin to blossom like heavenly flowers.

The evil one is busy at putting distractions in their path. The television is one of the biggest distractions. Many spend endless hours watching television, and afterwards, they are too tired to pray. They retire without giving thanksgiving to My heavenly Father Who loves them.

My child, share with your family that prayer is the spiritual food that nourishes their souls. Without prayer they are not aware of My heavenly Father. Prayer is the key to My Father's heart, for prayer leads to purity and holiness of heart.

You have a heavy cross, My child, in bringing your family and others to My Eucharistic Heart. Do not have any concerns, but trust Me. Continue teaching your family and others about the importance of prayer. Share with them that prayer brings about an interior change that leads to conversion. Share with them, that when they pray, they speak directly to My Eucharistic Heart. Now, My little child, be at peace and continue harvesting and cultivating hearts through your prayers and reparation.

I am Your Mother Come from Heaven to Love You

Message from Jesus in the Blessed Sacrament
February 25, 1994, 8:15 p.m.

Jesus
My dear child, welcome to My Eucharistic Heart. I, your Jesus of Love and Mercy, thank you for your efforts to come to be with Me. I know, My child, that you are suffering interiorly. Give everything to Me, and leave it with Me. I, your beloved Savior, want you to have no distractions that will take your attention away from Me. This time is ours. Speak to your beloved Savior. Pour out your heart to Me.

Janie
Oh beloved Jesus, I am all right. Sometimes, I get irritated when I am suffering. Please forgive Me for being such an infant. Help me to mature in my love for You and for my family. Help me to embrace my crosses without complaining. You know my heart, my Lord and my All. I only want to please You. Help me to be Your reflection in doing God's Most Holy Will.

Jesus
My little flower, how much you please your beloved Savior. It is because of your love for Me and your desire to do My Father's Will that you suffer. Never stop loving Me and continue to do My Father's Will, for your rewards are great in Heaven.

My child, be at peace, and allow Me to refresh your suffering heart. You are suffering for My sake, because you desire to live in complete holiness. This is a hard path to journey. You are doing well. Have no worry in your heart. My Father in Heaven is pleased with all your efforts. Be at peace, My child.

Janie
Thank you, my beloved Savior. I love you.

Jesus
I love you, My child.

I am Your Mother Come from Heaven to Love You

Teaching from St. Joseph, February 25, 1994

St. Joseph
Good evening, my little one. How are you doing tonight? I, St. Joseph, know that you are suffering. Tell me, how can I help you, tonight?

Janie
Beloved St. Joseph, I want to thank God for sending you to me and my family. We are so blessed! Glory be to God, forever and ever. Amen.

St. Joseph, I am sad, because my little son has been sick now, all week. I'd rather it was me instead of him, being sick. He is so special to me, and I hate to see him sick. I guess I'm just being a mother. I'm just down about having to work when my son is sick. I know that he is okay. Again, I'm just being a mother.

St. Joseph
My little one, you are a loving mother, who loves her child as you should. God is pleased with your concern over your child. You are a model of love and prayer to your family, and your family appreciates all your hard work and dedication to being a loving mother.

There are so many families that do not know how to love, because they do not take time to pray. Spouses take each other for granted and by doing this they become strangers to one another.

The word love has vanished from the hearts of many families. They don't have love in their hearts, because they do not know God. Only by praying will they discover God, and then love will settle in their hearts.

My little one, help me to intercede for all the families that do not yet know God. Let us pray together, so that tonight many families will be awakened to the love and mercy of God.

(We were silently praying together for all families).

My little one, you have been chosen to suffer in reparation for the hearts of families that live in darkness. God chose you because you are a loving wife and mother, and you have a generous and loving heart.

I am Your Mother Come from Heaven to Love You

Teaching from St. Joseph, February 25, 1994 (Continued)

Tonight, my little one, offer all your suffering in reparation for all children who suffer because their parents do not take the time to love them. There are numerous children throughout the world that grow up without love. These children suffer much, and they turn to others for love. Some children never find true love, for their parents have rejected their vocations to be loving parents. They have rejected God's gifts to them, which are their children.

Pray, my little one, pray and thank God with all your heart that you love your family. You are blessed by God for embracing your vocation as a wife and mother. I give you God's blessing. Remember, always, to be a loving wife and mother, and you will have God's total peace.

Janie
Thank you, beloved St. Joseph. Pray for my sons and for all families. I will also pray with you, I promise. Good night.

Message from Jesus in the Blessed Sacrament
February 26, 1994, 6:00 p.m.

Jesus
My child, welcome to My Eucharistic Heart. I, your Jesus of Love and Mercy, thank you for taking time out to come and spend time with Me.

So many of My children come to Holy Mass, but they do not stop by to greet Me. Many do not understand or believe in My True Presence. You console My Eucharistic Heart. I, your Eucharistic Savior, ask you to invite others to come and spend time with Me. Share with others how much I, Jesus, yearn to be with them.

My child, I have so many graces and blessings to bestow on those who respond to My invitation. I will refresh their heart and soul. I will make them strong, for I will be their strength. I have so much love to give all who come. I have so much love to give all who come! I will help them to unburden all their worries and anxieties. They will leave with peace and love in their hearts, for I am the Prince of Peace, and I am love.

245

I am Your Mother Come from Heaven to Love You

Message from Jesus February 26, 1994 (Continued)

<u>Janie</u>
My beloved Savior, I will bring others to You. I'll share what You tell me with them.

<u>Jesus</u>
Go in peace and let My love be your strength.

Message from Jesus. Our Lady was also present
In the prayer room, February 27, 1994, 9:30 p.m.

My Little Child,

I, your Eucharistic Savior, came to be with you, for I know how you long to be with Me, so I came to you. I know My child, that you gave that time up, so that you could be with your family. This is most pleasing to My Father.

My child, I am so pleased at your invitation to your husband to join you in your faith journey. It pleased Me that you offered your love and support to him and reassured him of your love for him.

You pleased Me in telling your husband that all you wanted to do was to be by My side and to love Me with every breath that you take. It was most pleasing to Me when you told him, that in loving him, you were loving Me. How very true you spoke to your husband, for it is in loving others that you love Me. My child, your words were filled with wisdom, and the Holy Spirit was speaking through you.

My child, you have pleased My Eucharistic Heart by sharing a special time with your husband. Share with other spouses the importance of spending time together and allowing My love to live in their hearts, so that they may love one another.

246

I am Your Mother Come from Heaven to Love You

Message from Jesus, February 28, 1994

My Child,

Today, I, your Eucharistic Savior, want to thank you for allowing My love to be your strength.

My child, you have been sharing in My suffering, and you suffer without complaining. You drink from the cup of My bitter Passion, and you drink it all with a loving and open heart.

My child, I want you to remember that no one in the world loves you more than I. Know that I am always with you whether you're happy or sad, whether you are with others or alone. I know your sorrows and your joys. I know everything about you, and I love you just the way you are.

My child, your wretchedness attracts My Eucharistic Heart. Your nothingness calls Me to bless you more, for I know that you are in much need of My love and My blessings.

Trust Me always, and I give you My solemn word that you will not regret it. Love Me always and allow no distractions to take you away from My love.

My love will lead you to complete holiness. I give you My word that your life will be transformed into My love if you put your trust in Me, your Jesus of Love and Mercy. Trust Me, trust Me now and forever.

I am Your Mother Come from Heaven to Love You

Message from Our Mother of Compassion and Love
February 28, 1994

LAST MESSAGE GIVEN BY OUR LADY FOR THE BOOK

My Little Angel,

How much you console my Immaculate Heart by following all the instructions given to you by Most Holy St. Joseph. Through his teachings you and your family have matured in wisdom and discernment. His teachings have brought your household many graces and blessings. Continue to live his instructions on the family and share his instructions with all my children.

My child, God so wanted to make your life complete in being a holy family, that He blessed you and your family with the visitations of Most Holy St. Joseph. Pray to God to give you the grace to be humble and obedient, like Most Holy St. Joseph. He is the model of humility and the obedient servant of God. Do everything that he tells you, everything!

My child, in just a short while your book with the teachings on the family will be published. This book will have a divine effect on all who read it with open hearts. Through this book many families will come to God as a family. The teachings in the messages given to you are teachings from Heaven, for God is calling all families to be reconciled to Him through being a holy family.

It is important that you pray to the Holy Spirit to prepare the hearts of the many families that will read your book. Prepare, my child, with strong prayer and fasting for the completion of the book. All my children who have dedicated their time and efforts for the completion of this book must pray and fast also, for Satan will attempt to disrupt my work in this book. That is why you must prepare every day with strong prayer and fasting for the success of my work in this book.

Trust me, my child, and do what I ask you to do. Pray to the Holy Spirit and consecrate the works of this book to Him, Who will bring my work to completion.

Trust me in my title of Mother of Compassion and Love, and allow me to teach you how to be the reflection of my Son, Who is compassionate and loving.

I am Your Mother Come from Heaven to Love You

Message from Our Mother February 28, 1994(Continued)

I am your Mother of Compassion and Love, Mother of the True God and Mother of All Humanity. I love you, my child. I love you.

I am Your Mother Come from Heaven to Love You

APPENDIX

AUTOBIOGRAPHY-Janie Garza

"Come to Me, all you who are tired from carrying heavy loads, and I will give you rest. Take My yoke and put it on you, and learn from Me, because I am gentle and humble in spirit; and you will find rest. For the yoke I give you is easy, and the load I will put on you is light." (Matthew 11: 28-30)

This Scripture reading has brought much comfort to me in my life journey, for I've come to know in a small way, how immense is God's love for me.

Today's date in June 23, 1994. It is two days away from the feast of the thirteenth anniversary of the apparitions of Our Lady, Queen of Peace, in Medjugorje.

Our Lord and His Most Holy Mother brought me here to this oasis of peace to write my autobiography. As I write, I pray to my Lord for the enlightenment of the Holy Spirit, for God knows that I am not a writer.

This morning while I was in prayer, Our Lady asked me to come to Apparition Hill (Podbrdo) to write my autobiography, and so I responded to her request. As I sit here next to the cross where Our Lady appeared to the six children of Medjugorje, my heart rejoices for the love that Our Lady has for all her children throughout the world.

I write in the love of Jesus and Mary to all the families in the world. I speak to the Church, to all priests and religious, and to the domestic families who will read these messages.

My name is Janie Garza. I live in Austin, Texas, and I am married. My husband, Marcelino, and I have been blessed with four sons, two grandsons and five granddaughters. In regards to my childhood, I was raised a Catholic, but I had no devotion to the Virgin Mary or to the saints.

As a child, I used to see my mother praying before her altar and lighting candles to all her statues. It seemed to me that she had every statue in the world. I used to resent her devotion, and seeing her praying to all the statues used to make me angry. I believed that she should pray only to God and stop wasting her time praying to statues! I was very young, and I didn't understand about devotions. My mother, being uneducated, didn't know how to explain to me about devotional love. She was a simple woman.

As I grew older, I learned to pray the Rosary all by myself, because Jesus was mentioned in these prayers. I had also read somewhere that the Rosary was a powerful prayer, and this appealed to me as a child.

I came from a family of nine children and my mother was the sole provider. We were very poor. I had a stepfather who stayed drunk all the time, and who was verbally abusive to the whole family. I couldn't understand why my mother stayed in this relationship.

I never knew my father. My parents separated before I was born. I remember how much my mother hated my father, and how angry she was with him, so she kept me from ever meeting my father. Because of my mother's anger towards my father, my mother was very abusive to me. She used to tell me that I looked exactly like my father.

As I grew older, it seemed to me that she resented me more and more. She used to tell me quite frequently, that I was adopted, and that's why I was very homely looking. This hurt me terribly, and it made me angry. As a child I remember suffering much and feeling very lonely.

I share this about being an abused child, because I know that many of you who read this book, you, too, have been victims of some sort of abuse. I remember that I loved my mother no matter how she treated me. In my own way I knew that she needed healing.

My mother never understood the importance of education, so she hardly saw to my education. The first year of education I went to first grade in a Catholic school. During this time the nuns taught me about Jesus in the Blessed Sacrament. I remember that, after school and whenever I could sneak in the church, I used to sit in front of the Blessed Sacrament waiting for Jesus to come out. I knew that He knew I was watching for Him. He never came out, but I never gave up on going and sitting before the Blessed Sacrament.

I didn't get to finish first grade because my mother took me out of school. She didn't tell me why, and I didn't get to make my first Communion. I did not understand the concept of not being able to receive Jesus until I made my first Communion. I felt such a love for Jesus that I walked to the church every day to attend Mass. I received Holy Communion, because I truly didn't know that I had to make my first Communion to receive Him.

I didn't make my first Communion until I was sixteen years old, but I used to attend Mass daily to receive Jesus. To me, He was my first real love. I feel in my heart that God forgave me for my ignorance.

As I grew up, I remember promising myself that I would never hurt anyone, because I didn't want anyone to suffer like I had, but that was the promise of a child. As I continued to mature in my life, I became very controlling of all the people in my life. I was very liberated in my morals and values.

When I married, I became worse. I wanted to wear the pants in my family, and I took charge of making all the decisions concerning our family. I didn't have the love or respect for my husband that I should have, so our marriage suffered.

I wanted equal rights, and many times I thought of divorce if things didn't go my way. It was at this point, that God in His love and mercy, sent Most Holy Mary into my life. God wanted to teach me to embrace my vocation as a wife and mother.

Our Lady first came to me on February 15, 1989. Her first words to me were on February 26, 1989. During this time Our Lady came to me every time I prayed my Rosary. She came dressed in white and gold with a huge Rosary.

At this time I thought I had lost my mind or that maybe I was working too hard. I was working as a supervisor in a psychiatric hospital, so I knew that I had to keep quiet about my experiences with Our Lady, or I would be committed as a patient.

I was well aware of the clients that I worked with and how they reported of seeing things or hearing voices. I was worried about myself, but when Our Lady would come to me, I was so at peace with myself.

255

AUTOBIOGRAPHY-Janie Garza (Continued)

On February 26, 1989, I had the courage to ask her who she was. Before speaking to her I sprinkled holy water on her to see if she was evil. She smiled. Then I asked her who she was and she responded, "I am your Mother come from Heaven to love you."

I asked her if she had a name and she responded, "To you, I come as the Lady of the Rosary. I charge you and your family to make living Rosaries for my son, Jesus."

I didn't understand what she meant. She said to me, "I, your heavenly Mother, will teach you on the virtue of obedience. I shall teach you how to be a loving wife and mother. I shall teach you how to be submissive to your husband." At this point I thought to myself, this isn't from God, because God knows that I am not a submissive person. I submit to no one!

Our Lady continued speaking to me: "Do not share with your family or others this special time that you spend with your heavenly Mother. I will tell you when to share with your family. Pray and fast for your family, so that their hearts will be prepared."

For five months, she came to me every day. Every day she would speak to me on how to love my husband. She was teaching the importance of praying for my family and how to embrace my vocation as a wife and mother. All that she asked of me, I held dear to my heart.

From all her teachings, I have been able to embrace my family one day at a time. She taught me not to dwell on the things of my past, not to worry about tomorrow, but to embrace God in the present moment.

To all who read this book, may the Holy Spirit inflame your heart with love for God and love for your family. Remember, your family is a blessing from God. Pray and trust God and give Him all your worries concerning your loved ones. He will take care of all your needs.

The best medicine to heal wounded hearts, to forgive, to convert, and to love your family and others around you, is prayer. Through prayer you will discover God and when you discover Him, you will know His peace.

AUTOBIOGRAPHY-Janie Garza (Continued)

Prayer is the fruit of the love of God; peace is His mercy. I pray God's blessings upon all who read these messages. Allow Jesus, Mary, and St. Joseph to guide you in your journey as a family.

For the past five years God has blessed our family with guidance from Our Lord Jesus, Our Holy Mother, and beloved St. Joseph. Now He will bless you and your family. May you and your family allow the love of the Holy Family to dwell in your home and in your hearts. God bless you all.

ACKNOWLEDGEMENTS- Janie Garza

No words in my heart could ever express my deep gratitude to all my beloved friends, especially Kathie Caspary, whose tireless dedication and perseverance brought to completion this book, my past spiritual directors who helped me and guided me in a loving way, and to my parish Pastor who has been so supportive.

I am most grateful to my present spiritual director, Fr. Henry Bordeaux, O.C.D., who encouraged me and gave me hope when my spirit lagged and whose prayers and sufferings gave me strength.

I extend my gratitude to the prayer group of Our Mother of Compassion and Love, for all their love, prayers and support. Special thanks to Lucille, Jan, Mary, and my dear soul mate. I love you all. I am deeply grateful to all these beloved people for their unique contributions.

Most of all, I extend my deepest gratitude to my Blessed Mother, who came from Heaven to love me and my family, and to my Lord and Savior for His immense love.

Janie Garza continues to receive messages from Jesus, Mary and St. Joseph. Our Lady will advise Janie when the remaining messages are to be published.

LETTER FROM VICKA

Since 1981, Our Lady has been appearing to several individuals on a daily basis in a small village in the south-western Croatian area of former Yugoslavia (now Bosnia-Herzegovina). While in Medugorjie for the Thirteen Anniversary of the apparitions, Janie Garza met with Vicka Ivankovic, (one of the original Apparitionists, now 30) who continues to visit with Our Lady. Vicka sent the following letter to Janie following the meetings and conversations they shared.

Bijakovici, June 27, 1994

Our Lady, is, in a special way concerned *about young* people, families, and peace. The young people are in a very, very difficult situation. We can *help them with our* love and prayers from our hearts.

This is *the time* of great graces. She wishes that we come back to her messages and that we begin to live them with our whole heart. Our Lady is praying for peace and she is inviting us to pray for her own intentions and that we help her with our own prayers .

Vicka

See the next page for a copy of the actual letter

Bijakovići, 27.06.94.

Gospa je na poseban način
zabrinuta za mlade, Obitelji, Mir.
Da se mladi nalaze u jako jako
teškoj situaciji a da im mi
jedino možemo pomoći našim
Ljubavlju i molitvom srca.
Ovo je vrjeme, vrjeme velike
milosti, želi da obnovimo njezine
poruke i da i počnemo srcem
živjeti.
Gospa mali za Mir pa poziva i
nas da ini molimo za istu
njezinu nakanu i da joj
pomogemo našim molitvama.
Vicka

Letter from Vicka to Janie

260

INDEX

TOPICAL/WORD INDEX

The following is a topical or word index to many of the key words of the messages. This index is provided as a helpmate in referring to the messages.

264

Printed in the USA by

Z'Atelier® Publications
Plano, TX 75023-1710

Picture of Janie Garza, 1994, Austin, Texas

Mother of Compassion and Love
Artist: Jaunita Farrens, New Orleans